MADAM SECRETARY

ALSO BY THOMAS BLOOD

*State of the Union: A Report on President Bill Clinton's
First Four Years in Office*

MADAM SECRETARY

A Biography of
Madeleine Albright

by
THOMAS BLOOD

St. Martin's Press   NEW YORK

A THOMAS DUNNE BOOK.
An imprint of St. Martin's Press.

MADAM SECRETARY: A BIOGRAPHY OF MADELEINE ALBRIGHT.
Copyright © 1997 by Thomas Blood.

Design by Jenny Dossin

Library of Congress Cataloging-in-Publication Data

Blood, Thomas.
Madam secretary : a biography of Madeleine Albright / Thomas Blood
p.   cm.
ISBN 0-312-17180-3
1. Albright, Madeleine Korbel.
2. Women cabinet officers—United States—Biography.
3. Cabinet officers—United States—Biography.
4. United Nations—Officials and employees—Biography.
5. Ambassadors—United States—Biography.
I. Title.
E840.8.A37B57   1997
327.73' 0092—dc21
[B]   97-16521
CIP

First Edition: November 1997

10 9 8 7 6 5 4 3 2 1

To my three wonderful reasons

for living: Debbie, Sean, and Kelli

CONTENTS

CONTENTS

ACKNOWLEDGMENTS

First and foremost, I want to thank my dad, Col. Thomas Blood (1917–1997), my best friend, who departed this world when I was halfway through this project. He spent his whole life fighting the enemies of democracy so that people like Madeleine Albright could live in freedom. Also, I want to thank my beautiful mother, who always wanted me to be a writer, and the rest of my great, big, fantastic, Irish-American family.

I want to thank my dynamo of an agent, Jenny Bent, as well as my publisher, Tom Dunne, and St. Martin's Press. Also, I wish every author could experience the keen insights and support of my world-class editor, Peter Wolverton. Pete, "You Da Man!"

Anyone familiar with the project knows that the book simply wouldn't have gotten done without the help of the incomparable Eric White. Thanks, "Swami."

Several others were instrumental in the completion of *Madam Secretary* and deserve special mention. They include my Eastern Europe advisor Glen Hicks, my research assistant Beckett Dickerson, Lauren Battaglia, Steve Powell of the law firm of Holland and Knight, Leon Billings, Jim Davidson, Peter Krough, Elliott Levitas, Lindsey Lewis, Kevin McDonald, Kristen Nardullo of St. Martin's Press, Randy Nuckolls, Geraldine Ferraro, and Senators Patrick Leahy and Barbara Mikulski.

I would also like to thank Dawn Alexander, Robert Budway, Tom Burgess, Ken Carlson, David Carrol, Chris Duda, Scot Freda, Quay Hays, Paul Henry, Chris Kersting, Ken Markowitz, Kimerly Montour, Jim Nader, Beverly Perry, Steven Pruitt, Ann Rowan, Michael Schwartz, and Kris Van Geisen for their ongoing friendship and support. Special kudos to the techno-wizards at OnTrack Data Systems and Novatron who rescued the project from computer hell so many times. Finally, a thousand thanks to Tommy Jacomo at the Palm, Jon and Luis at Market Street, and to the crew at the Reston Starbucks, all of whom put up with me and my laptop for hours on end during the writing of *Madam Secretary*.

I couldn't have done it without you.

OVERVIEW

This is the story of Madeleine Albright, the most dynamic woman to come along in politics since Margaret Thatcher. If 1992 was the Year of the Woman, and 1994 was the Year of the Angry White Male, then 1997 was unquestionably the Year of Madeleine Albright.

From her childhood escape from the Communists to her critical role in the Bosnian Peace Accords, to becoming the first woman to serve as this country's Secretary of State, Albright's life story appears like that of many lives rolled into one.

As her biographer, I became convinced early on that

proper treatment of the subject necessitated more than simply chronicling the events of her extraordinary life. Rather, to truly gain insight into Madeleine Albright the person would require going behind the scenes, getting the perspective of those who knew her then and now on a professional and personal level—in short, talking to the people whose lives she impacted directly.

Accordingly, rather than employing a traditional "birth to death" method in telling Albright's story, I have identified ten "defining moments," or periods, in Albright's life that best open a window onto the Secretary of State's uncanny ability to triumph over adversity and her unparalleled success in politics, as well as her meteoric rise to dominance in the world of foreign policy.

It is important to understand that this treatment is not presented chronologically but, rather, much like a tapestry, tying key experiences in Albright's career and personal life together in the hope that the reader will get some measure of the woman who is leading American foreign policy into the next millennium.

I

POWER PLAY

Winning the Nomination

as Secretary of State

It was 10:01 P.M. EST on November fifth. Election Day, 1996. Most of the polls on the West Coast had just closed, and ABC anchor Peter Jennings, speaking on behalf of the network, was reporting that exit polls in Ohio projected that the Buckeye State had pushed the President over the top, that Bill Clinton had been reelected as this country's forty-second president. To UN Ambassador Madeleine Albright, this was a moment of both great triumph and tremendous relief. For Albright, who had been at the President's side from the very beginning, this campaign had become rather personal. The President was not only her boss, but also her close friend. During the last four years, she had watched him weather a constant onslaught of attacks from his opponents. Despite the Republican blitzkrieg, she and others had done their best to fulfill the administration's agenda. Some days were better than others. More often than not, Madeleine Albright had held her own better than most.

Now, at least for the moment, there would be a reprieve. The President, as the first Democrat to be elected to a second term since FDR, would have a few weeks to bask in the sunlight of his victory. Even better, the night was still young. Before the polls closed in California, the potential margin of victory still held out hope for a mandate. But for now that was not important. A win was a win. Period. As Albright sat on the couch in the living room of her spacious $27,000-per-month penthouse apartment in New York's tony Waldorf Towers, she turned to her longtime chief of staff and confidant, James P. Rubin. With the glee of a teenager at a homecoming game, she remarked, "Never a doubt. Never a doubt."

Then the phone began to ring.

The first call came from Little Rock, but it was not the caller Albright was expecting. It was Washington power broker and Clinton confidant Vernon Jordan, who, as part of the President's inner circle, had flown a private jet to the Arkansas capital to be with the Clintons in their hour of triumph. "Madeleine, it's Vernon Jordan. What are you still doing in New York?"

Albright was curious. Although she and Jordan were friendly enough and shared a professional respect for one another, he had never called her at her New York apartment before, out of the blue, just to chat. And it was election night no less. Something was up, she thought. "I've been asking myself the same question all night," she responded. "Unfortunately the UN doesn't just shut down because of the American elections. You're in Little Rock, I take it?"

"That's right. At the Excelsior, with the President."

"So how's he doing?"

"Glad it's over. Very, very glad it's over. . . . He's exhausted."

"I'll bet."

"Listen, Madeleine. Let me tell you why I'm calling. The President has already asked me to head up the vetting team at the State Department. Assuming you're interested, I think it would be a good idea for you to connect with White House personnel and begin the process. . . ."

By "vetting," Jordan was referring to the exhaustive personal background check conducted by the FBI that all presidential appointees must undergo. And, even though she had been vetted four years earlier for her appointment as ambassador to the United Nations, she understood that the process must be repeated for each new appointment. What was unclear was whether she was going to be offered the top job at State or whether she was just one of many candidates in contention. The ambiguity stemmed from the fact that during its first term the Clinton administration had run into trouble with some of its appointments, announcing them publicly before the FBI background checks were complete. As happens, some background checks routinely take longer than others, particularly when a nominee has extensive financial holdings. In Washington, however, any delay in the vetting of a candidate, for whatever reason, can prove embarrassing, even fatal to a nomination. In light of this, about midway through the first term, the White House took corrective action, issuing a directive that candidates for all positions needed to be thoroughly vetted before the White House would even acknowledge that they were under consideration.

While Albright wanted to come right out and ask Jordan directly if there was a short list, she held back. For weeks her name had been mentioned along with three or four other candidates to fill the top spot at Foggy Bottom, yet no clear front-runner had emerged. And despite the fact that clarification of her status would have been welcome, she resisted. Vernon Jordan was a first-class pro, if there ever was one. To ask him if there were others on the list would put him in an awkward position. No, the fact that he had called at all told her how fast things were moving. "Thanks for the heads up."

"Don't mention it."

"Give my best to the President and the First Lady."

"You know, Madeleine, it might not be a bad idea if you made that call yourself," he said, subtly making the point that the President would like to speak with her.

"Okay, Vernon. I can take a hint. I appreciate it," said Albright as she hung up.

No sooner had Albright put down the phone than another call came in. This time it was from longtime friend and ally, Senator Patrick Leahy from Vermont, a stalwart

Clinton supporter on the Foreign Relations Committee. Leahy, calling from his home in Burlington, said, "So, Madeleine, how does it feel to be employed for another four years?"

Albright stood up, walking across her spacious living room to the balcony, taking the phone with her. As she took in the view of the East River, she said, "You know something I don't, Pat? What's the buzz?"

"Yeah, I know that if we don't get to work, this train's gonna leave without you," said the senator in stark terms. "The clock is ticking." Leahy paused for a second, and then continued. "And by the way, aren't you supposed to be in Little Rock?"

"My bag has been packed for two days. I'm still trying to find a USAir shuttle between New York and Little Rock," she said facetiously, referring to her well-known reputation for flying the New York–Washington shuttle almost daily in order to protect her power base both at the United Nations and in the White House. "Someone's got to mind the store."

Nothing in Albright's answer surprised Senator Leahy. She was as committed a professional as he had ever met. While the other contenders in the race for Secretary of State had formulated well-conceived plans to campaign for the nomination—some had even hired publicists and thousand-dollar-an-hour public relations consultants—Ambassador Albright had done exactly what anyone who knew her would expect. With the vital issues of the world being debated every day on the floor of the General Assembly, with the human rights of millions at stake, Albright characteristically put duty before career and had yet to consider the matter seriously. Leahy, who, in addition to his senatorial duties, was a delegate to the International Conference on Land-Mine Decommissioning, was scheduled to leave the next day on a fact-finding mission to China, so he said, "I'll be back from Beijing in a few days. What are the chances I can talk you into meeting me in Washington over the weekend? We can sit down with some of our brain trust and map out a strategy. I'll set it up. . . ."

Given Albright's single-minded determination and occasional tendency to become fixed on the challenge at hand, she was grateful to have friends like Leahy to jolt her into action mode when necessary. "I thought you'd never ask," she said.

If Madeleine Albright had yet to consider exactly how she would go about becoming Secretary of State, she had expended no shortage of gray matter contemplating what she would do if ever handed the job. Only weeks earlier, Senator Leahy, having received confirmation that then Secretary of State Warren Christopher was indeed stepping down, challenged Albright. Playing the *what if game*, he posed questions like, What if you were Secretary of State? What would you do? What would you seek to change? Much to Leahy's surprise, Albright did not resist. Instead, over a dinner of grilled rockfish and penne pasta she gave him chapter and verse on what the United States and the State Department needed to accomplish during the next four years, spelling out her worldview in no uncertain terms, emphasizing her vision of the United States as the "indispensable nation."

It was at that moment that Leahy became certain that, whether or not his old friend understood how to go about getting this job, she was better prepared to assume the mantle at State than he had expected. That night, Leahy returned to his hotel room and wrote in his diary, "This country would be well served if Madeleine Albright was the next Secretary of State."

Indeed, Leahy had no idea how long Albright had been preparing for this very possibility. From the first day of her tour as the US Permanent Representative to the United Nations—a job she openly professed to love—the ambassador was quietly planning the next step of her meteoric career. By all accounts her rationale was simple: "The more power and influence one has, the more one can do to help people."

Toward this end, Albright briefly toyed with the idea of seeking elective office, following the lead of another highly regarded UN envoy, Daniel Patrick Moynihan, by running for the Senate. But, as the immigrant child of a diplomat, she'd led a near-nomadic existence for most of her life and lacked a real home state from which to mount a Senate race. Absent that option, Albright instead focused on doing what was necessary to elevate the stature of her post as the American UN ambassador. If she was ever to have a chance at the top job at Foggy Bottom, she needed to act the part. Step one was booking a travel schedule that looked like that of a Secretary of State. Knowing that frequent flyer Warren Christopher tended to focus on the major capitals of the world, Ambassador Albright decided to take what was left. While Christopher was shuttling between London, Paris, Bonn, Tokyo, Tel Aviv, Riyadh, and Damascus, Albright made a point of visiting the capitals of dozens of countries otherwise ignored by State's more senior diplomatic contingents. This included such exotic locales as Nairobi, Baku, Kinshasa, Port-au-Prince, Tbilisi, Tiranë, Mexico City, Lima, and Santiago.

In shoring up her diplomatic credentials, she was also building political capital with the dozens of envoys throughout the world. But she didn't stop there. Albright made a special point of becoming intimately acquainted with her essential foreign policy partner, the military, rarely missing an opportunity to court key members of the armed forces. When US troops were stationed in Somalia, she went to Mogadishu. Wanting to witness the Bosnian civil war herself, she made a similar trek to Sarajevo. When her schedule permitted, she accompanied Joint Chief Chairman General John Shalikashvili, visiting US troops overseas. Adorned in a Day-Glo orange life vest, helmet, and goggles on the deck of the aircraft carrier *Constellation*, smiling a big grin, as the American flag flapped in the wind overhead, Albright showed once again that she is the master of the photo op. Having flown into war zone after war zone, the self-effacing Albright reflected to *Time* magazine on the one great revelation yielded by her travels.

"You know what I discovered about myself that I did not know? It's that I'm not afraid. I've done what I need to for my family. My daughters are the greatest source of pride for me—but they don't really depend on me anymore. I have a great sense of freedom now."

This statement itself is rather extraordinary coming

from a person born to up-and-coming Czech diplomat Josef Korbel in Prague in 1937. Her family escaped the Nazi invasion of Prague when she was an infant and later, when she was eleven, they fled her native Czechoslovakia in the dark of night under the threat of a death sentence imposed on her father by the new Communist regime.

No city on Ambassador Albright's travel schedule was more important than Washington, D.C., however, where she felt compelled to attend the regularly scheduled weekly cabinet meetings as well as the National Security Council principals' strategy sessions. The triple designation as UN ambassador, cabinet member, and National Security Council member had proven to be both a blessing and a curse. On the one hand, Madeleine Albright wielded what former Reagan envoy Jeane Kirkpatrick characterized as "power of unprecedented proportions, both at the United Nations and at the White House." On the other hand, circumstances required that, to protect her turf, she often had to be in two places at once.

Before election night was through, the phone rang several more times for Madeleine Albright, with calls coming from former vice presidential candidate Geraldine Ferraro, Maryland Senator Barbara Mikulski, and close friend and antiquing buddy, Barbra Streisand. Making the acquaintance of the world's most famous diva was one of the truly unexpected benefits of Albright's position as this country's permanent representative to the United Nations. But, as both women will attest, theirs is much more than a casual business friendship. Despite the vast pressure on their schedules and intense public scrutiny to which both were subjected, the two women had developed a genuine friend-ship. The truth was that Albright found Streisand an in-credibly warm and loyal friend. As she said to her staff more than once, in her business "a gal can't have too many of those." The feeling is apparently reciprocal, as Streisand is fond of telling people, "We just became instant friends. We talk about everything: love, relationships, a lot of pol-itics."

As the night wore on, every caller had the same thing on his or her mind. For Madeleine Korbel Albright there would be at least one more shuttle to Washington to pro-tect her turf. But what neither she nor Senators Leahy and Mikulski, Geraldine Ferraro, Barbra Streisand, or the rest of her brain trust knew at the time was whether it would be the last.

No sooner had Albright arrived back in Washington than the clock, in Senator Leahy's words, began to tick. Early on, Leahy, who served as point man spearheading Albright's nomination, was able to learn that the selection of a new leader for the foreign policy team had divided the White House into two competing camps. One camp con-sisted of outgoing Chief of Staff Leon Panetta, Senior Ad-visor Bruce Lindsey, and Clinton-Gore Communications Director Anne Lewis. The other camp, referred to inter-nally by administration officials as the "Corporate Board," due to the Wall Street slant in their thinking, included Vice President Al Gore, incoming Chief of Staff Erskine Bowles, Treasury Secretary Robert Rubin, and Vernon Jordan. Of-ficially, the First Lady was out of the loop on the nomi-nation, but was thought to have exercised considerable influence on the process in direct discussions with the President.

Not surprisingly, the two camps favored very different candidates. Leon Panetta, who saw himself as the architect of the new foreign policy team, viewed its selection as his last, most important accomplishment as chief of staff. Accordingly, he had become steadfast in his belief that whoever was chosen to take over at State should be a person whose worldview was compatible with Bill Clinton's. Panetta first came to know the President as his director of the Office of Management and Budget and later replaced Mack McLarty, taking over the chief of staff position, heading up a hopelessly demoralized White House staff after the 1994 election debacle. During his two years as COS, Panetta had come to learn some surprising things about the President. First, Bill Clinton is a man of enormous intellect who regularly has a better grasp on issues, no matter how obscure, than even his most senior advisors. It was commonplace during the first term for an aide or even a cabinet member to spend weeks preparing a briefing only to be ripped to shreds by a President who characteristically reviewed the briefing book only an hour before, yet somehow committed its entire contents to memory. "The President is so smart, it's scary," says one top White House official who requested anonymity. Not surprisingly, with Clinton's confidence in his advisors marginal at best, an instinctive need to control every aspect of the White House operation was born early on. By all accounts, this trait dates back to his Arkansas days. In fact, for much of his first four years the President was the de facto political director, domestic policy advisor, and budget head.

Contrary to the allegations that he was a poll-driven politician with no political center, the President, in Panetta's view, was a man of deep political convictions. His problem wasn't that he didn't stand for anything, but rather, that he constantly fought a battle with his own insatiable need for control. One area where he was able to exercise restraint was in foreign policy. After all, Arkansas was not exactly a mecca for international trade. To the President, it only made sense to defer in geopolitical matters to more learned, experienced minions such as Warren Christopher. Despite the logic of this thinking, Panetta knew that this mentality had gotten the President into trouble during his first term, notably in Somalia. Over a period of months, after taking hit after hit in the media, the President began to ignore the counsel of his cadre of elder statesmen and war heroes such as Colin Powell. Instead, he began to follow his gut, relying on his own instincts, reaching out to advisors who shared his worldview. In short order, things began to click. Panetta knew that on the heels of the foreign policy successes in Haiti and Bosnia, the President was beginning to gain confidence in international relations and would undoubtedly continue to be his own chief foreign policy designer. In short, that would require someone at Foggy Bottom who shared the same vision as the President. As discussions ensued with factions from every wing of the Democratic party and the foreign policy community weighing in, only one consensus candidate continued to surface: UN Ambassador Madeleine Albright.

For Albright, that was the good news. The bad news was that the Corporate Board had other ideas. In fact, a number of sources confirm that some of its members were conducting an "anybody but Albright" campaign inside the White House.

Within days the battle lines were drawn. Collectively, the Board, led by Bowles and Rubin, backed the selection of former Armed Services Committee Chairman Sam Nunn, with former senator and majority leader George Mitchell as a second choice. Jordan sought to talk up the strengths of all the candidates. Vice President Al Gore was the lone dissenter, solidly giving his support to Special Envoy Richard Holbrooke, the often brilliant, sometimes volatile negotiator of the Bosnian peace accords. As for Madeleine Albright, her name was absent on the short lists of every member of the Board.

As for the Board's three short-list candidates, each had strengths and weaknesses. One of the Corporate Board's primary concerns was that the nominee carry some weight with the Republican-controlled Senate. In this regard, Senator Nunn proved a formidable choice. Though a Democrat, the senator from Georgia had considerable clout among his GOP colleagues, as well as a reputation as a foreign policy hawk, which endeared him to many in Europe. Another big plus: Nunn was a Southerner, and despite the President's reelection, when it came to the South, the White House still needed all the help it could get. On the downside, Nunn had long been a critic of the President. His penchant for drawing stark contrasts between their views and approaches to policy dated back to their days as succeeding Chairs of the Democratic Leadership Council. Nunn was fond of saying about the President that he "has been a bright, young rising star in three different decades."

Former Senator George Mitchell's problem was not a relatively scant résumé in the foreign policy arena. The bulk of the former majority leader's experience consisted of service as the special negotiator on Northern Ireland on behalf of the administration and the chairmanship of the International Crisis Group, a privately financed organization that facilitates nonviolent solutions to conflicts around the world. Despite the brevity of his foreign policy experience, Senator Mitchell still impressed many on the Hill and in the media. His performance as the chief envoy to the Northern Ireland Disarmament Conference still rated rave reviews. The problem with Mitchell was more than that. While no one would say so officially, there was no love lost between Mitchell and Foreign Relations Committee Chairman Jesse Helms. In fact, the two had been fierce adversaries for over a decade. Moreover, a high-level committee source told the White House that while he was in the Senate, George Mitchell wasn't known for playing fair, that he'd burned too many bridges, that many of his colleagues in the supposedly collegial body were out to get him. In short, the source told the White House, Mitchell's nomination was "dead on arrival."

The Vice President took a particular interest in promoting the candidacy of former Assistant Secretary of State for Europe, Richard Holbrooke. Gore's people emphasized Holbrooke's credentials—he had negotiated the Dayton Accords that led to the Paris treaty on Bosnia, often bringing a Kissinger-like toughness to the job. Besides that, Holbrooke was media-savvy, which they argued would be a welcome change from the reticent Warren Christopher. But like Nunn, Holbrooke had his flaws. His detractors noted that his roughshod style rubbed many in the administration the wrong way.

Thus, the Board's short list read like a casting call for *Grumpy Old Men*, with all three being white males in their fifties, with reputations ranging from being difficult to work with to being downright neurotic. And while no one could argue that Nunn, Mitchell, and Holbrooke lacked the qualifications for the Foggy Bottom post, none possessed enough of the qualities needed to transcend the various factions inside the White House. The problem, as Panetta had tried to warn them, was that no matter how much support a candidate had, the President still had to be convinced the selection would be a good fit. It wasn't long before the Board, sensing frustration and indecision on the part of the President, began to submit second-tier candidates to Clinton. This group included Undersecretary of State Strobe Talbot, an Oxford roommate of the President when they were both Rhodes Scholars, former Vice President and ambassador to Japan, Walter Mondale, and of course the unsinkable General Colin Powell. Yet still no mention of Ambassador Albright came from this camp.

By the end of the first week no decision had been reached and rumors continued to circulate throughout the city. One had it that State was George Mitchell's post for the asking. Another posited that the President planned on appointing former Senator William Cohen and Ambassador Albright to a joint secretariat, a concept that had pundits and constitutional scholars shaking their heads. Again the Powell rumor surfaced, and, contrary to popular belief, Vice President Gore not only didn't oppose the nomination, but had become its biggest proponent. Convinced that mustering support for the Holbrooke nomination was next to impossible, Gore began seriously to consider Powell at State. Well aware that his closest advisors were more than leery, some say downright terrified, at the prospect of elevating his likely opponent in the 2000 presidential race to the level of this nation's senior diplomat, Gore nevertheless pressed for a fair hearing on the issue. By all accounts, after a long and grueling campaign, the Vice President had grown weary of the selection process. His argument, in essence, was that sometimes you simply have to put politics aside and just do what is in the best interest of the country. Notwithstanding the impact of such an appointment on his own electoral chances in 2000, the Vice President insisted that if Colin Powell was the best candidate for the job, then so be it. Suffice it to say that such thinking had Gore's handlers pulling their hair out by the roots.

The debate raged on in the Old Executive Office Building throughout the weekend, until one top advisor saw a silver lining to a Powell appointment. In strictly political terms, the logic was undeniable. By taking the high road, the Vice President would appear unthreatened, even presidential, even if Powell declined the nomination. But if Powell accepted, then the general would no longer be able to attack the administration without consequence. Even better, when it came time to seek the Republican nomination for President, Powell couldn't very well attack the policies of the very White House in which he served. Effectively, he would have become part of the problem. Thus, even though they were coming from diametrically opposite points of view, on Monday the Vice President and his senior advisors threw their support behind a Powell nomination.

As it turned out, the real reason Powell's candidacy stalled was that the President had simply grown sick of him. During his first term, Clinton had made countless overtures to the general to join his administration and had been rebuffed each time. It didn't help that Powell had irked the President by openly campaigning for Bob Dole as well as recounting private conversations with Clinton—supposedly held in confidence—in his memoirs.

During the next few days several events unfolded to Albright's advantage. First, out of nowhere Senate Foreign Relations Committee Chairman Jesse Helms weighed in, giving his strong support to Ambassador Albright. More than that, Helms went the extra mile, informing the White House which candidates would make it through the committee and which ones would not. The fact that the senior senator from North Carolina went to bat for Albright came as no surprise to his staff, which was well aware of his soft spot for the UN envoy. For instance, Helms wasn't shy about his feeling of kinship with his fellow die-hard anti-Communist. When her name came up in conversation, the senator seized any opportunity to boast of his admiration for her role in the ouster of UN Secretary General Boutros Boutros-Ghali and for the way she dressed down the Cubans. He was particularly fond of recalling the time in 1994 when French Defense Minister François Léotard had alleged that the US was exaggerating the military threat posed by Iraqi strongman Saddam Hussein. On the floor of the General Assembly, Albright had given her typical, tough-as-nails performance, accusing Léotard of "giving comfort to a brutal dictator who is a repeat offender." She'd gone on to say that the French government's policy toward Iraq had been less harsh as a result of its commercial interests in Baghdad. Countless sources attest to the fact that the Helms-Albright relationship is more than merely professional, with several of their colleagues recalling the time that the senator called on Albright in New York to ask if she would consider flying to North Carolina to speak at a luncheon for a foundation near and dear to his heart. Ambassador Albright agreed to attend the luncheon, but on one condition: "All I ask is that you come on down and introduce me."

As for the luncheon, the two spent most of it carrying on like long-lost sweethearts. Helms even went so far as to play the role of waiter, presenting her with the entire dessert tray, referring to himself as her humble servant. The luncheon's hostess, Elizabeth Fentress, commented that by the time the senator escorted Albright to the airport later that day they looked as if they were on a date.

The second major development came when several key players in the women's movement began pressuring the White House on the nomination. Individually, Senators Barbara Mikulski, Dianne Feinstein, and Barbara Boxer all called the President. Connecticut Representative Barbara Kennelly called Gore directly, making it clear to the Vice

President that Clinton's unprecedented level of support among female voters was not automatically transferrable to him. Former vice presidential candidate Geraldine Ferraro bypassed all of them, choosing instead to play intermediary between Albright and the First Lady. It was in these discussions that she learned that Vernon Jordan had quietly warned Albright that campaigning too openly for the job would destroy her chances. Ferraro, well aware of the aggressive campaigns being waged by Albright's opponents, was outraged. This had all the signs of a classic Washington setup.

"Did Vernon tell you to your face that he was going to make your case to the President?"

"Not exactly."

To Ferraro, it didn't add up. "Then it's bullshit," she exclaimed, not nearly as trusting in Jordan's neutrality as Albright.

Albright, for her part, was torn. Friends like Ferraro counseled her to move aggressively, to adopt a take-no-prisoners approach. On the other hand, Health and Human Services Secretary Donna Shalala and other allies were adamant that Albright not be seen as self-promoting, campaigning for the job. "Your fingerprints can't be anywhere near this one," Shalala warned. "Keep your head down and stay cool." Shalala's admonition struck a chord with the ambassador, compelling her practically to beg key figures in women's groups not to campaign for her, fearing a backlash from the Foreign Relations Committee.

As pressure began to mount, Albright exhibited tremendous restraint, telling herself over and over again that she loved the UN job, that if State wasn't meant to be, it wasn't meant to be. She went as far as telling her senior staff that if the President asked her to stay put at the UN, she would gladly remain, with no complaints. "It is way beyond any of my dreams," she remarked. "God willing, life will go on."

And then it happened.

It was late Monday, around 6:30 P.M. Throughout the day, administration press secretary Mike McCurry had been hounded during press briefings about the timing of the appointments. Several members of the White House press corps, including CNN's Wolf Blitzer, reminded McCurry that the President had promised his new national security team would be named before week's end. But that deadline had come and gone. McCurry was resolute that, notwithstanding the delay, he had nothing new to report. Progress was being made, he informed them, but no decisions had been finalized as yet. So, absent any substantive developments, the press corps began to stalk anybody and everybody with a White House business card in a quest to find out what was happening at Foggy Bottom. Normally, the staff at the Clinton White House, a notorious sieve, was about as tight-lipped as Howard Stern. But not this time. Uncharacteristically silent, the staff was not talking because quite frankly, very few people were actually in the loop on this one. This went on for almost an entire day. But finally, as the deadline for the networks grew closer, the long-awaited sound bite came. A highly placed, unidentified White House official, speaking on condition of anonymity, explained that Albright was out of the running, that the White House had viewed the UN envoy as a second-tier candidate all along.

By 6:41 P.M. the story aired on ABC *World News Tonight.* By 6:44 P.M. the White House switchboard was lighting up like Macy's windows at Christmas, so flooded with calls that the lines began to roll over to the auxiliary lines in the Old Executive Office Building. One White House source said the last time they'd seen anything like this was when the President announced the administration's ill-fated "Don't ask, don't tell" policy regarding gays in the military. By seven o'clock the White House was in full damage-control mode, with McCurry and Communications Director Don Baer convening a crisis management meeting in the Cabinet Room that included Vice President Gore's top flack Lorraine Voles, as well as Clinton-Gore Communications Director Anne Lewis.

The stakes were astronomically high. For the President, who had been reelected with a seventeen-point margin among women voters, alienating this critical voting bloc was akin to political suicide. But there was no getting around it. The damage had been done. As a result of the leak, the President had suffered a crisis of confidence with the primary constituency that had gotten him reelected. The severity of the rift could not be overstated. To say that tension was running high between the White House and women's groups was a lot like saying that Woody Allen and Mia Farrow were having a minor disagreement over child-rearing. Not since the split with labor over NAFTA had the White House suffered such a serious setback with a core constituency group. Within a matter of minutes, the

White House saw its relationship with female voters hit rock bottom. Perhaps diminutive Senator Barbara Mikulski, a close friend and staunch supporter of Albright's, put it best. "It was like Kazzam! An insult to all of us," said the senator. "But the good news was it gave us a chance to launch a full-court press."

Over the next several days, the pro-Albright forces did just that. By Monday the first item on Vice President Gore's calendar was a meeting with representatives of a coalition of sixty women's groups to talk about what role women, family, and workplace issues would play in Clinton's second term. They also met with other key White House officials, including personnel deputy Patsy Thomasson, to discuss procedures for applying for jobs. But Gore, seeing the gap between this key voter bloc and his own presidential aspirations growing ever wider, did not stop there, and made arrangements to meet with a women's advisory panel sponsored by the centrist Democratic Leadership Council by week's end. What's more, the Vice President instructed Voles to distance him from the position of the Board. In the statement, Gore rejected the remark suggesting that Albright was a second-tier candidate, saying that Albright's potential candidacy would be considered on its merits. Voles went on to add, "He doesn't think Madeleine Albright is a second-tier anything. He has enormous respect for her."

As for Madeleine Albright, she was experiencing a rare case of nerves. She spoke at length with good friend Ferraro, expressing her fear that even if the lobbying effort on her behalf proved successful, her stature at State would be diminished if the appointment was turned into a quota. In response, Ferraro, Mikulski, and others advised her not to worry, that the White House had so mishandled her situation that no one would dare make such an allegation. Moreover, they assured her, even her opponents acknowledged privately that on paper Albright was far and away the most qualified candidate for the job. Senator Leahy concurred, adding that as to the gender issue, the genie was out of the bottle, that the White House, a.k.a. the Board, had painted itself into a corner and would be playing defense for the rest of the game.

Even so, Ambassador Albright, not a person accustomed to inaction, was feeling restless. It was completely against her nature to sit back idly and do nothing. Late into the night, she and Leahy pondered the question of what could be done to affect the process. Finally, it dawned on the senator. As a result of the inadvertent leak, the issue of gender had taken on a disproportionate level of importance in the debate. Predictably, battle lines were drawn, with feminist groups going on the attack and a small, yet extremely powerful contingent of white males circling the wagons as things heated up. It was Leahy's position that it would be in Albright's interest to shore up support from potential unnatural allies.

Taking Leahy's advice, Albright began to reconsider the strengths of some of the competition. In short order, she focused her attention on Sam Nunn. In taking a closer look at the former senator and chairman of the Armed Services Committee, she concluded that, in addition to impressive credentials in the areas of defense and foreign policy,

Nunn's strongest selling point was that he was acceptable to a large bloc of very conservative Republican senators. With this in mind, Albright wasted no time contacting longtime friend and Reagan administration alum Ken Duberstein. Having made arrangements to meet at a black-tie dinner later that evening, the two took time out for a sidebar. There, in the main ballroom of the Ritz Carlton, while a big band played Tommy Dorsey in the background, Duberstein echoed support for Leahy's strategy. "If you can line up the senatorial Republicans," he began, "the White House won't know what hit 'em." As Albright listened intently over the din of the music, the longtime GOP operative explained that the only way to corral them was retail politics. In other words, good old-fashioned arm-twisting.

The good news, reasoned Duberstein, was that Albright already had Jesse Helms on her side. The bad news was that there were roughly another twenty Republican senators who hated the State Department, who hated foreign aid, but most of all, they hated the United Nations. Upon hearing this, Albright was encouraged. Despite her stationing in New York, she knew enough about the Clinton administration's congressional relations shop to know that long-term planning was never its strong suit. She would bet even money that not a single phone call had been made to any of the Republicans on the Foreign Relations Committee to get a measure of the leadership's mind-set on State. While part of this could be explained by the fact that the Senate could conceivably have changed hands on Election Day, Albright knew in her gut that it had more to do with simple incompetence. Like it or not, the administration had a certain style when it came to nominations. The term *advise and consent* was not exactly part of the White House vocabulary. Rather than attempt to work out honest differences concerning a nominee, a far more likely possibility had the White House hedging its bets, going for the sure thing, that is, selecting someone it was confident the Senate likes as opposed to asking what they think.

With this in mind, Madeleine Albright went to the Hill, and began a door-to-door lobbying campaign, listening for hours to Republican hard-liners such as Rod Grams of Minnesota, Craig Thomas of Wyoming, and Rick Santorum of Pennsylvania, go on chapter and verse about Somalia, China, and Boutros Boutros-Ghali. The process went on for days, with the envoy gaining not just a few supporters, but pulling off the greatest mass conversion since Henry VIII reformed the Church of England.

Another convert to the pro-Albright camp was Republican foreign policy maven Jeane Kirkpatrick, who, in addition to serving as UN ambassador during the Reagan administration, had been the chairwoman of Republican presidential nominee Bob Dole's election campaign. Ironically, had Dole won, Kirkpatrick would have been well positioned for an appointment to State herself. On Albright, Kirkpatrick went on record, saying, "I hope if Bill Clinton is reelected, he'll appoint Madeleine. I'd like to see a woman in the job."

Meanwhile, down at the other end of Pennsylvania Avenue, the President, completely unaware that Albright had lined up every GOP senator behind her, was getting closer to a decision. He had been openly disdainful of the media's suggestion that the UN Ambassador had been eliminated from consideration, and notwithstanding what others in the White House may think, Madeleine Albright was always on his short list.

While those on his senior staff could not be sure, the President appeared in the view of many to be sending a signal. True, early on he had sung the praises of George Mitchell, to whom he had grown close during their time together rehearsing for the debates when Mitchell played the role of Bob Dole. But Clinton had also been vocal in his support for Albright's talents, often remarking that "she gives the best public articulation of my foreign policy of any person around." Throughout the selection process, the President recalled Senator Mikulski's assessment of Albright: "A lot of diplomats may grasp the complexities of Bosnia, but only Albright could explain why we were there in a way that the local grocer could understand."

Publicly, the first real sign that the President was leaning toward Albright came when Vice President Al Gore not only broke ranks with the Board, but took great pains to distance himself from their thinking, issuing a statement that Ambassador Albright was his first choice all along. Still, there was no official confirmation. Other than generally giving Albright a vote of confidence as his favorite foreign policy spokesperson, the President had been unusually closemouthed on the subject, as had the First Lady. Even so, Mrs. Clinton was widely rumored to be Albright's staunchest supporter. Her reticence on the subject was largely attributed by administration officials to a malady commonly referred to in the West Wing as "health care hangover." Recalling the unprecedented partisan wrangling and attacks that resulted from the First Lady assuming the high-profile role as head of the Health Care Reform Task Force, her advisors saw no percentage in publicly injecting her into the selection process. The truth was that Hillary Clinton desperately wanted to see Madeleine Albright get the top post at State, but after years of taking more than her fair share of cheap shots, the First Lady reasoned that discretion was the better part of valor, and decided to work on Albright's behalf behind the scenes.

For the next several days Albright held round-the-clock consultations with her brain trust, conferring with Leahy, Mikulski, and Ferraro in Washington and New York, and via phone with Streisand. Leahy, who had had several Oval Office discussions on the nomination, was firmly convinced that the only candidate that President Clinton supported was Albright. He was also convinced that the President was actively looking for political cover. In other words, the more people like Leahy, Mikulski, and Helms who jumped on board the Albright bandwagon, the easier it would be for the administration to sell the nomination.

Finally, on Tuesday a break came when the President called, catching Albright in her Manhattan apartment, just as she was running out the door. The two spoke for several minutes, with the President telling Albright how exhausted he was from the campaign, about how much he, Hillary, and Chelsea were looking forward to their vacation as soon as all the major appointments were decided. At that moment, Albright later told friends, she thought the

President was about to offer her the job. For several seconds there was a pregnant pause. As the awkward silence continued, Albright didn't know whether or not to start talking, change the subject, or come right out and ask the President about Foggy Bottom. The ambassador, far from a wallflower, quickly decided that now wasn't the time to raise the subject. Bill Clinton was her friend. If he was going to offer her the job, he was going to do it on his own schedule. In all probability this call was simply to take her temperature, or to see if there was any residual resentment from the second-tier rumors.

Just when the silence was becoming embarrassing, the President changed the subject himself, asking Albright about the health of her close friend, Czech President Václav Havel. For several more minutes the two chatted, telling jokes and swapping stories about the days leading up to the President's reelection. But still no offer. Finally, the President, apparently interrupted by a staffer, thanked Albright for all her help and abruptly ended the call. To say that this left the ambassador frustrated is an enormous understatement.

On the positive side, the efforts of the women's group appeared to be working. Rumors began appearing in every major newspaper that the tide had turned in her favor, that her appointment was imminent. The new problem raised by this shift in momentum was that Albright began to get inundated with congratulatory calls and telegrams. Unfortunately, she was in the uncomfortable position of telling them that, yes, she had heard from the President, but that, no, there had still been no offer.

When Albright surmised that the President was going to take his sweet time in deciding on State, she had no idea how right she was. Tuesday dragged on into Wednesday, with the President taking advantage of the unseasonably warm Washington weather to contemplate his options during a round of golf at the Army-Navy Country Club. The President had grown unbelievably attached to the hilly, par 71 course, located just minutes across the Virginia state line, in Arlington. Taking off in the middle of the workday, a stressed-out President could be on the first tee in less than ten minutes via presidential motorcade. With the Secret Service cordoning off the holes in back and in front of the commander in chief, effectively sandwiching the President, Clinton would often play two or three balls at a time, giving new meaning to the expression, "slow play," often driving members crazy. Longtime Army-Navy member Robert Budway, a one handicap and a Washington trade association executive, describes playing behind the President as about as brisk as watching a balanced-budget amendment move through Congress. Several old-timers joke that they haven't seen a sitting President play this much golf since Ike. But, in the President's defense, he has gone on record many times saying that the solitude of playing Army-Navy affords him the opportunity to collect his thoughts and sort out his options when he needs to make a difficult decision.

Apparently this time it worked.

Later that evening, just after nine o'clock, during a holiday ball at the White House, outgoing Chief of Staff Leon Panetta was interrupted while dancing with his wife and summoned to the kitchen in the mansion. "I think I'm near a conclusion here," said the President.

"Should we ask Madeleine to stop by?" asked Panetta.

"No, not just yet." responded the President. "But track her down in case I need to speak with her."

After Panetta left, the President headed for his private study, a magnificently decorated room, filled with mahogany cabinets and shelves holding a library of signed first editions of works by Twain, Faulkner, Hemingway, Churchill, and John and Bobby Kennedy, and with the walls adorned with dozens of candids of past presidents. He sat down on a leather couch and took out a legal pad and began to scribble the names of the people on his own short list, jotting down a few last-minute remarks on each one's strengths. For the President there had always been only two choices, former Senator George Mitchell and Madeleine Albright. Others in the White House may have had their candidates, but Clinton had remained unmoved. He was restless, having agonized all day about the decision. The round of golf was therapeutic, he was about 90 percent there. Over and over he thought about one senator's warning about Mitchell's chances. The last thing he wanted to do was to go through what happened to George Bush with his Defense nominee, John Tower. Bush had won election handily, only to be humiliated by the resounding defeat of the Tower nomination, which left his presidency permanently wounded, a wound from which Bush never quite recovered. No, President Clinton would be damned if he was going to let that happen. So, as he had many times in the past, he turned to his most trusted advisor, his wife. Fortunately for Albright, the First Lady told her husband exactly what he needed to hear. "Forget about what your advisors think," was her advice. Knowing that the President had been genuinely puzzled by the lack of support among his advisors for Albright's nomination, she pressed him to follow his instincts. "Trust your gut, Bill," she told him over and over again.

Shortly before going public with the selection, the President placed a phone call to a longtime ally now serving in a diplomatic post in the Middle East. The purpose of the call was to take one last poll of an old friend on the selection of Madeleine Albright. The call was made from the study and lasted about ten minutes. By the time it was over the President was wringing his hands. His trusted friend had been blunt. Madeleine Albright was totally qualified to serve as Secretary of State, but he couldn't support her. He told the President that the majority of the trouble spots on the geopolitical landscape were in the third world. And most of these were Islamic nations. Their leaders would never take her seriously because she was a woman.

As the President sat there contemplating the thought of Madeleine Albright in deep negotiations with Hafiz Assad of Syria, he placed yet another call to Panetta, who told the President that the ambassador had caught the last shuttle back to New York. "Should I have her return tonight?" asked Panetta.

The President knew that at this time of night—it was almost eleven o'clock—short of dispatching Air Force One to bring her back to Washington, his options were limited. "No, but schedule a call on a secure line for first thing tomorrow. And, Leon, set the appointment yourself. I don't want the staff gossiping about this."

In the early hours of Thursday, December 5, *the call* finally happened. Panetta, taking no chances, asked Albright to grab the 6:00 A.M. shuttle back to Washington, just in case the President wanted to see her in person. Reaching Albright at her Georgetown town house at 7:46 A.M., the President wasted no time, telling her that while she had his support, some members of the diplomatic corps had strong reservations concerning her ability to deal with the third world, particularly Muslim leaders. While his tone was serious, he tried to lighten the subject by joking about her making a "no *cojónes*" speech at the Dome of the Rock.

Characteristically, Albright didn't miss a beat. "You know what they say, Mr. President," she said. "They can't cut 'em off if you don't have 'em."

Her retort broke both of them up, truly easing the tension. The President, amazed once again at her unflappable manner, asked her, "So you really think you can handle the likes of Assad?"

"Are you kidding, Mr. President. Compared to Jesse Helms, that guy is a puppy dog."

With that, the deal was done. "Okay. You got it," said the President.

2

POWER BRUNCHES, POWER LUNCHES, AND SALON DINNERS

There is an old saying in the nation's capital that when it comes to politics, nothing ever happens by accident. In this vein, much has been made of Madeleine Albright's meteoric rise to power, particularly the period during the 1980s, when as a university professor, she is alleged to have turned her posh five-bedroom Georgetown town house into a virtual state department "in exile," a high-powered salon that regularly attracted the best foreign policy minds in the city. It was in this setting, so the story goes, that Albright hosted numerous dinners and cocktail parties through which she built her network of supporters in the diplomatic community. This exclusive group included ex-State Department officials, journalists, academics, and politicians.

Moreover, if rumors were to be believed, Albright's salon was considered a regular stopover for foreign dignitaries visiting the Reagan and Bush administrations. If a state dinner was being held for Israeli Prime Minister Shimon Peres on a Thursday, he was likely to dine at the two-story, red brick, federal-style Albright home on Wednesday. Then–British Prime Minister Margaret Thatcher is said to have been a regular whenever she made her way to the States. Thatcher, notorious for, among other things, her bouts of jet lag whenever she flew from London to Washington, is said to have prevailed upon her hostess on more than one occasion to change plans from dinner to brunch. By all accounts, Albright was only too glad to accommodate the Iron Lady of the UK, typically throwing together last minute meals of poached eggs, English bangers, biscuits, and currant jam. And it has been reported that not every meal was of the gourmet variety. Take the time that Queen Noor of Jordan, who, when in town usually stays only a few blocks up the road from Albright at the Park Hyatt on Twenty-fifth Street, decided, without warning, to pop over. The good news was that a senior lobbyist from the Wine Institute had arrived about an hour earlier with a case of vintage Cabernets under one arm. The bad news was that no one had given any serious consideration to the menu. So, for the next several hours Queen Noor joined Albright and several guests as they dined on delectable fare that included Hamburger Helper and Pringles, washed down by several bottles of 1985 Opus One. Of course, it wouldn't be Washington without dinner guests openly attempting to generate spin on the evening, some of whom referred to the entree jokingly as Le Helper.

The fact that Madeleine Albright made her tony Georgetown town home available to legions of foreign policy wonks during the 1980s is not in dispute. Neither is the fact that for more than a decade her guest list included some of the most prominent and influential individuals in Washington, D.C. But what has been reported rather inaccurately by the media is why the so-called salon dinners occurred in the first place. The line in the popular press was that Albright relished playing the role of foreign policy maven of the Democratic Party, and that she loved the home field advantage of having a virtual brain trust of international relations gurus pass through her revolving door on a weekly basis.

In point of fact, the so-called salon dinners never occurred. Sure, there were lots of dinners, cocktail parties, and retreats at the family farm in Berryville. But, contrary to common belief, they were never intended by Albright to cultivate support or build a power base. Ironically, one of the best kept secrets in town was that the real reason for the dinners was that there was no reason. They happened quite by accident and coincidentally filled a void in the Democratic political community. To hear Peter Krough, dean emeritus of the Walsh School of Foreign Service and longtime Albright pal, tell it, "Madeleine was about as far away from a 'salon dinner type' as you could imagine. She was incredibly down to earth, outgoing, just so glad to have you in her home. These so-called salon dinners would be more accurately described as colleague dinners. Rather than catering to an exclusive power elite, it was simply her 'circle of friends.' " And what a circle she had. Several sources attest that among Albright's comrades were, at any given time, half the sitting cabinet, dozens of senior embassy officials, every top academician in the city, and several Democratic presidential candidates, as well as literally hundreds of Georgetown University students.

The attraction was rather simple. For twelve years the Republicans controlled the White House and at least one house of Congress. Democrats in Washington had become a virtual enemy camp. Other than the budget, they were by definition excluded from any proactive positioning when it came to policy making. Nowhere was this more striking than in the area of foreign relations. So with most of the Democrats in town having adopted a siege mentality, many, in the words of former Muskie Chief of Staff Leon Billings, "Simply needed a place to go. A place to interact and exchange ideas with their colleagues." In hosting roughly a thousand such gatherings over the course of a decade, Albright not only provided the venue, but was personally responsible for the spiritual restoration of many of her colleagues. Not spiritual in a religious sense, but more in the way a tremendous athlete can inspire dejected teammates to reach down deep inside, to play harder, and come from behind to victory. "No matter what the occasion. No matter how tough the challenge, Madeleine was always upbeat. She never, ever lost her sense of humor," says Billings. "It was easy to get down in those days," says Washington lobbyist Jim Davidson, "but Madeleine absolutely refused to admit defeat." Another colleague put it in even starker terms. "The world was changing rapidly—the Middle East, Nicaragua, Tiananmen Square, not to mention the first hints of glasnost. People's lives were at stake, and we were all sitting on the bench, unable to affect any of it, to make any sort of contribution. But Madeleine refused to get discouraged. More than that, she refused to let you get discouraged either."

On a professional level, to the extent that a substantive theme ran through the dinners, it involved Albright's work in the 1980s first as the Vice Chairman of the National Democratic Institute for International Affairs, and later as the head of the Center for National Policy. The NDII was an offshoot of the National Endowment for Democracy, a foreign policy brainchild of Democratic power brokers Chuck Manatt and Peter Kelly. Manatt was Chairman of the Democratic National Committee during the grim period following the Reagan defeat of Jimmy Carter, and is widely credited for introducing major innovations and reforms that were responsible for the party's very survival during the 1980s. Recognizing that the Democrats would be relegated to a back bench role until such time that they regained power, the National Endowment was set up as a nonpartisan funding mechanism to facilitate participation in the formulation of American foreign policy by individuals from across the ideological spectrum. On the left was the NDII headed by Albright, which included on its board such heavyweights as eventual Clinton cabinet members Warren Christopher and Robert Rubin, as well as her ex-

boss, former senator and Secretary of State Edmund Muskie. On the conservative side was the International
Republican Institute, which took a decidedly different view
of things.

For several years the NDII was funded solely by the
National Endowment, including the publication of widely
respected studies on emerging democratic movements. But
perhaps the most notable achievement by the NDII was
acceptance of NED-certified election observers in pivotal
1988 elections in Nicaragua pitting candidates backed by
the Contra rebels versus the Sandinistas. At long last, after
years in exile, the Democrats were finally having some effect. Albright's hardworking never-say-die attitude continued until 1989 when Kirk O'Donnell stepped down as
president of the Center for National Policy. Following the
counsel of Billings, Davidson, and others, Edmund Muskie
asked her to take over the organization. That Albright was
a competent executive and effective administrator came as
no surprise to anyone who had ever worked with her. That
she had, within a matter of months, completely transformed the organization in every way—from fund-raising,
to research, to basic philosophy, surprised even her biggest
supporters. She is credited with redirecting the emphasis of
the research team from an academic style of research to
one embracing a cutting edge methodology relying heavily
on polling and public opinion research in their analysis.
With more than a little pride, Albright coined the concept
"internistic."

By the time Albright had finished her first year at CNP,
every key Democratic senator in Washington was calling

her, knowing that she and her staff had a much better handle on the vital foreign policy issues of the day than did their respective staffs. On any given day, she would be hammering her staff to deliver the definitive analysis of some major international issue, having promised the Center's white paper to the ranking member of the Senate Foreign Relations Committee, and by nightfall she would have had her entire research team, as well as the ranking member's entire staff, over for potluck. "The Center for National Policy was extremely important to Madeleine," says Billings. "Not only was it a pivotal logical next step in her professional evolution, but it gave the Democrats an intellectual policy standing in the foreign relations arena, opposite the Heritage Foundation and AEI. She gave it life. Not only that, she breathed life into Ed Muskie," who after the Carter defeat, was left without any real platform from which to speak out on the critical issues facing the country. "In the course of turning the Center into a viable and effective organization, Madeleine developed an enormous degree of credibility with a host of Democratic senators and congressmen who would prove absolutely essential to the next stage of her career." A prime example of this has been Albright's relationship with current House Minority Leader Dick Gephardt. Gephardt, when asked about Albright is quick to emphasize that "Madeleine is more than just my colleague, she is my friend." He goes on to speak glowingly of their many hours working on joint projects together when Albright was head of the Center for National Policy and he was House Majority Leader, particularly their fact-finding trips to Eastern Europe around the time of the fall of the Berlin Wall. "She just has this in-credible people sense," says Gephardt. "Back then, while most of the congressional delegation was walking around West Berlin pondering the strategic impact of the collapse of East Germany, Madeleine was reminding everyone of the human component of this radical change, that people, especially children would be enormously affected by the reunification of the two Germanys and that the US had to be ready to step in with humanitarian aid if necessary." And then there was the time in 1990 that Gephardt was preparing to deliver a tough, bare knuckles speech to the Polish-American Chamber of Commerce in Chicago at-tacking then-President Bush's policy regarding Poland. At the last minute he asked an aide to send the speech Al-bright's way for a quick read through. Within the hour she had returned the speech to Gephardt with her suggested revisions along with a note explaining each change. "The truth was that I had all the facts straight as well as all the strategic arguments down. But what I had no way of knowing was the individual perspective, what it must be like to be a Pole, living under that kind of oppression, or for that matter, to be a Polish-American with family living back there. Madeleine gave me the refugee's perspective. Making me understand what it was like to live under that kind of a government. I will never forget it." The speech, incidentally, was a rousing success.

To hear Billings and other longtime colleagues tell it, Albright's knack for building these types of relationships and coming through in the clutch, "was not calculated, but it wasn't unplanned either. Madeleine always took advantage of the situation in which she found herself." And, while this ever-growing network of relationships may have seemed like a good move politically, one never quite knew who might show up at Albright's door. One eclectic gathering took place on a summer evening in 1988, roughly a month before that year's Democratic National Convention. Albright herself had been appointed a member of the DNC's platform committee and had been hard at work on several foreign policy planks that defined the party's stance on arms control, human rights, and covert aid to the Nicaraguan Contras. And while any number of issues were floating around Washington that summer, there was no stated purpose for the dinner, other than the fact that Albright had received a call earlier that day from Chuck Manatt, who said a young friend of his was in town and that she should meet him. It so happened that the young friend was the governor of a small Southern state and that he had recently been tapped to deliver the keynote speech at next month's convention in New York. The young man's name, Manatt told her, was Bill Clinton.

For Albright, any recommendation by Chuck Manatt was gospel. After all, Manatt, in addition to his stints as cofounder of the NED and party chair, was generally known as the consummate Washington player, heading the most powerful lobbying shop in the city. But more than that, Chuck Manatt was a dear friend. Any endorsement from his mouth carried significant weight in Albright's book. "What does he like to eat?" asked Albright.

"He's not coming by for the food, Madeleine. He's coming because he wants to meet you," said Manatt.

That evening Manatt and Clinton showed up fashionably early, around seven-thirty. After a few quick hellos, Manatt, who owned interests in several vineyards back in California, retreated with Albright to the kitchen to help with the wine. Temporarily abandoned Governor Clinton wandered about the Albright home. Classically furnished with pieces reflecting the federal period of the home's construction, it was quite colorful since the walls of every room were filled with bright oils and pastel hangings. As Washington lobbyist Peter Kelly described it, "Tastefully decorated. Expensive but not fancy. So cozy you don't want to leave." Evidently, Clinton thought so, as he eventually made himself at home in Albright's parlor. Spying a copy of that Sunday's *New York Times*, he immediately began to search for the crossword puzzle. About this time a few guests began to trickle in, one of whom was an old college classmate of Clinton's from Georgetown. He describes the following scene: From the foyer, he could see Clinton sitting alone in an easy chair as Albright, ever-present diet Coke in hand, emerged from the kitchen to let the governor know that more guests would soon be arriving. She also asked if she could get him anything. Ever the Southern gentleman, Clinton rose to his feet and, not wanting to impose, insisted that he was fine. "I'm all set," he is quoted as saying, holding up the blank crossword puzzle.

Despite the fact that Clinton was the perfect low-maintenance dinner guest, Albright felt it necessary to fetch her guest a glass of wine. As soon as she exited, Clinton dived into the puzzle. After ten minutes, Albright returned, wine goblet in hand, apologetic for taking so long. As she set the glass down at a nearby table, she appeared astonished to see that the young man in her easy chair had already completed the entire Sunday *Times* crossword puzzle in less than ten minutes. Upon returning to the kitchen, she is said to have remarked, "Chuck, that is one smart guy in there."

Without looking up, Manatt said, "You haven't seen anything yet. Wait till you meet his wife." And so began the political and intellectual courtship between Madeleine Albright and the man who would someday be President.

That evening, Albright, Manatt, and Bill Clinton, along with a dozen or so guests, consumed ample portions of London broil, pasta salad, and expensive red wine as they discussed a wide array of topics that included the never-ending Iran-Contra investigation, Gorbachev's tenuous hold on power in the Soviet Union, and the potential list of running mates for George Bush—the consensus had it that Paul Laxalt was a shoo-in. Then the subject turned to the upcoming Democratic Convention, and Clinton's speech. As they discussed any number of potential themes, some asked the young Arkansas governor what he would do if Michael Dukakis, the Democratic nominee, asked him to join the ticket. Clinton, after nearly choking back his wine, took a deep breath and said with a straight face, "Aw heck. I've never even thought about running for President."

As the night wore on, the party retreated to Albright's spacious backyard. One of the biggest in Georgetown, it is long—roughly a third of an acre—and is filled with plush trees and thick shrubbery. Albright is reputed to be an avid and skillful gardener, yet due to her schedule, she rarely has the chance to sip a glass of lemonade in her garden let alone work in it. Seated around a regular wooden picnic table under a moonlit sky, the group sipped coffee as Albright and another guest entered into a spirited discussion involving whether or not continued US funding of the Contras would have any real effect on Nicaragua. Notwithstanding the fact she ran a Democratic think tank and that most of her friends were left-leaning Democrats, everyone knew that Albright was a staunch anti-Communist. While she didn't love the Contras, she detested Manuel Noriega and the Sandinistas. More than that though, she was incensed that the Soviet Union and Cuba were playing nation-building in the backyard of the United States. And while she, like most Democrats of that period, opposed funding the Contras, it was more on the basis of their reported brutality and attacks on Nicaragua's civilian population than due to ideology. Some of her guests disagreed, saying they couldn't support the Contras under any circumstances. With the discussion at an impasse and becoming just a tad unfriendly, Bill Clinton chimed in, "You know, in a way, you're both right."

Albright, who wasn't aware that the state of Arkansas was any particular hotbed of geopolitical activity, was curious to hear what the affable young governor had to say on the subject. His words struck a permanent chord with her as he reasoned that the United States absolutely could not sit idly by while the Soviet Union or anybody else sought to make inroads in areas that had been traditionally within the American sphere of influence or in which it had a vital strategic interest. The problem, he explained, was not opposing Soviet and Cuban expansionism, but the Reagan administration's favored course of using proxies and covert funding to defend US interests.

"What do you propose, that we send in US troops to Managua?" snapped one guest.

"What makes you think they aren't already there?" said Clinton in return.

"So, Governor, what is your position? Do you support the Contras or not?" asked one of Albright's former students who showed up at the last minute.

"I support being honest with the American people. If there is a vital interest of the United States being threatened, then our leaders have an absolute obligation to stop that threat. And that includes military intervention if need be. But at the same time our leaders have just as strong an obligation to inform the American people on what the threat means and who will be doing the fighting."

So as the evening wound down, the contentious discussion evolved into friendly conversation on such subjects as the nuclear freeze movement, the European Green Party, the precarious hold on power of the ruling coalition in Israel, and somewhat surprisingly, saxophone music. Somehow, in this eclectic group the only saxophonist was the man from Little Rock, who seemed to enjoy going on at length on the musical stylings of Stan Getz and Dave Brubeck. Madeleine Albright would later tell friends that the dinner had been a great success, that she'd met this impressive young governor, a bright, handsome man who was a comer. As Albright would say to friends, Clinton had written her a three-page thank you letter for dinner. In the letter, he mentioned his desire to join the Council on Foreign Relations in passing, almost as an afterthought. Over the next few months the two exchanged correspondence and several phone calls. Finally, Governor Clinton came right out and asked Albright for a recommendation to the Council on Foreign Relations. And while she was more than impressed with the young man's intellect and verve, the foreign policy maven of the Democratic Party felt she needed a better sense of the governor's position on several key foreign policy matters before she could endorse his nomination to the Council. Playing the role of Svengali, she suggested that Clinton put some of this thoughts down on paper, that he write her a quick memo on such subjects as Afghanistan, Angola, Northern Ireland, and glasnost. What Albright expected was a short but sweet memo drafted by a staffer, written under the Arkansas governor's signature. But what she received instead was a 120-page treatise exploring each issue in excruciating detail. As Albright said to one colleague, she had no choice but to recommend Clinton. "I just didn't have any time to read any more memos," she said.

Despite Albright's jokes about her early meetings with Bill Clinton, the informality of the setting, and the spontaneity of the hostess, the real significance of the salon dinners during those years cannot and should not be underestimated. It was no accident that a young governor who would, to the surprise of many, be elected president in 1992, sought to forge a strong and trusting relationship with Albright. In truth, however, the scenario repeated itself many times over the course of a decade, involving over a dozen major political figures who made the pilgrimage to the foreign policy mecca located on the shady Georgetown street. Senator Bob Kerrey, who unsuccessfully sought the Democratic nomination in 1992, made Albright's home his first stop as he assembled his team of campaign advisors. The same can be said for Senators Joe Biden, Tom Harkin, and Paul Tsongas. Notwithstanding Albright's stated position of neutrality—necessitated by her affiliation with the Center for National Policy—every Democratic candidate in 1992 actively courted her support. And according to Kerrey, "Every single one of us met with her and every single one of us came away certain that she liked us best." But it didn't start there. Going as far back as 1984, Albright's counsel has been coveted by any number of politicians contemplating a run for the top job in politics. Geraldine Ferraro likes to tell the story that after receiving the vice presidential nomination in 1984, she made the mistake of not listing foreign policy as one of her strong suits. As the media seized hold of this apparent weakness, Ferraro's good friend Barbara Mikulski didn't mince words, telling her in no uncertain terms to meet immediately with Albright. By 1988, after being pursued by a group that included Mario Cuomo, Ted Kennedy, and Dick Gephardt, Albright became the top foreign relations advisor to Democratic presidential nominee Michael Dukakis.

In short, whether the salon dinners were completely spontaneous events devoid of any identifiable agenda or a carefully orchestrated series of group therapy sessions designed to position Albright as the nucleus in the Democratic foreign policy molecule is really not important. What is significant is the end result. It is clear that between the years of 1980 and 1992 whoever was destined to lead the Democrats in their battles to regain the White House would inevitably have passed through Madeleine Albright's door. There they would break bread, hoist a glass of spirits, and share their vision of the world with the woman who would come to symbolize this nation's foreign policy.

And then, of course, any discussion of Albright's salon dinner period should touch on the true salon dinner to end all salon dinners. About two months after Albright had been confirmed as UN Ambassador, she hosted one of her fancier parties for her close friend, Czech President Václav Havel. Havel, a Nobel Prize–winning playwright and human rights activist had known Albright since his days as a dissident under the thumb of the Communist regime in Czechoslovakia during the late 1960s and '70s, about which Albright wrote her doctoral dissertation. Not surprisingly, the two stayed in close touch over the years, with Havel requesting that Albright serve as his advisor and translator during his first trip to the United States in 1989. Now several years later, with Havel having ascended to the presidency of the newly formed democratic Czech Republic, Albright wanted to throw a party for her friend that would simply redefine hospitality. According to close friend and colleague Gail Griffith, Albright spent weeks planning the event, sparing no expense, wanting every detail to be perfect. As the date approached for Havel's visit, in late April 1993, Albright grew increasingly anxious, checking every menu item again and again with the caterer. As for the guest list, it was, for weeks, one of the best-kept secrets in town. So guarded was the list that invitees, including the President and the First Lady, were asked to deny any knowledge of the affair. This was done for several reasons: one was to minimize hurt feelings among Albright's endless circle of friends. "Anyone who knows Madeleine understood that she would have invited half of Washington if she could have," said a close friend, "but her house is only so big." The second reason was to avoid tipping off the media. After all, it was supposed to be a surprise party for Havel. As one might guess, with the advance teams, Secret Service, and assorted embassy security details involved, keeping the lid on this event was next to impossible.

By the time guests began to arrive, word had started to leak out to the media. As for the event itself, everything went like clockwork: the food, the wine, the music. It was approaching ten o'clock, and everyone—Albright, Havel, the President included—was having a blast. Albright was beaming with pride. Amazingly, she'd thrown a near-perfect party for her dear friend and she had pulled it off discreetly. But unfortunately, as neighbors spied the Presidential motorcade parked out front the die was cast. It was time for dessert and the Washington press corps was descending upon Albright's Georgetown abode. The carefully orchestrated affair, the sole purpose of which was to allow a few old friends to have some quality time with one another outside the glare of the media spotlight, was about to be invaded by the media. Or so it seemed. The fact was that for weeks Albright had anticipated this and had other ideas.

With little or no explanation, Albright summarily announced to her guests that they were all heading off-campus for dessert. The first to leave were the President and First Lady, who had been advised of the destination about an hour before. Then, as the press began to gather outside, the guests dispersed in five-minute intervals, all heading for the preselected rendezvous site. The last to leave were Albright and Havel, the guest of honor, who had been kept in the dark the entire time. For about twenty minutes, the two sat in the back of a limousine as the chauffeur followed the most circuitous route imaginable to the next stop, with Havel's security detail following close behind. Finally, satisfied that the press had gone home for the night, Albright instructed the driver to head down an alley between Wisconsin Avenue and Thirty-fifth Street to Washington's premier jazz club, The Blues Alley.

As the two walked past a line of two hundred people to the entrance of the club, they were met by manager Ralph Camilli, a longtime fan of Havel's writings. Camilli, a savvy veteran of the music business who rubs elbows with top names in entertainment every day, could hardly contain his excitement as he welcomed the Nobel prize-winner. Havel, by all accounts, was moved beyond words by Albright's surprise. The fact was the Czech president had been a lover of jazz since his dissident days when he and his friends would ever so carefully smuggle 45 rpm records of such artists as Louis Armstrong, Scotty Mc-

Donald, and Billie Holliday into Communist-dominated Prague. Why 45-speed records instead of albums, Havel was often asked. "Because they were easier to hide," he would answer. Little did he know that the best was yet to come. Understand that Havel, for all of his profound intellect, did not speak or read English well enough to discern from the marquee who was waiting inside.

Together, the two walked arm in arm down the stairs into the smoky club. Once inside, after their eyes adjusted to the darkness, Albright just stared as her close friend took in the scene. Albright had arranged for the entire party—including the First Family—to relocate to the Blues Alley, not just for dessert, but to witness an extraordinary moment. She would have been happy to have performed introductions but was confident that there was no need. As Havel approached their table, located only a few feet from the stage, he couldn't believe his eyes. Seated on stage was hot young guitar virtuoso Kevin Whitfield, perhaps the best jazz guitarist in the business and one of the costars of Havel's favorite American film, Robert Altman's *Kansas City*.

"Mr. President. Welcome to America," called out Whitfield.

Havel, in a mild state of shock, looked at Albright and in a heavy Czech accent said, "Madeleine, is there anything that you haven't thought of?"

As for Ambassador Albright, she just smiled a self-satisfied smile, having gotten the reaction that she wanted from Havel. He had traveled a long way. She wanted him to feel welcome. Apparently her plan was working.

For the next two hours, Whitfield put on one of his strongest performances for a unique audience, which boasted two presidents, a secretary of state, two ambassadors, three senators, and a former vice presidential candidate. But on that night in the spring of 1993, the only thing that mattered to Madeleine Albright was that they were her friends and that they were having a good time.

Meanwhile, back at Albright's upstairs office in her home, her fax machine was ablaze, as letters and messages continued to come in from major capitals around the globe, in dozens of different languages, offering best wishes to the UN Ambassador and welcome to Václav Havel. This would go on for hours, well into the night, until her fax machine ran out of paper.

3

Coming of Age

The Georgetown Years

It was raining around 7:30 A.M. that Wednesday morning and Madeleine Albright could not have been happier as she sat behind the wheel of her 1980 Datsun 280ZX sports car for the first time in days. Even though winter was fast approaching, Washington had been unseasonably warm for over a week, offering her little excuse to drive to work given the fact that she lived less than three blocks from her office at Georgetown University's Walsh School of Foreign Service. Dr. Albright, as she was called by her graduate students in comparative government, had always prided herself on knowing the difference between work and play. As for her shiny, copper-and-black, 180-horsepower, high-performance vehicle, it came, fully equipped with AM/FM cassette player, T-Top sunroof, and power everything. It definitely fell into the category of play and was the envy of every undergraduate at Georgetown. Unfortunately, given that there were only so many hours in a day, Albright rarely got to drive her elegant ride, as she called it jokingly, more than a couple of times a week. But after going six days without wheeling the Z down the Clara Barton Parkway along the Potomac River, enough was enough. So, that morning, while every other Washingtonian dreaded the bumper-to-bumper commute amid the gray drizzle falling on the nation's capital, Albright gunned the engine and pulled out into traffic, taking the long way—that is, another six blocks down M Street, to Georgetown University. As she pulled into the faculty parking lot, the attendant couldn't help but smile as he saw the diminutive Albright—all of five feet tall—turning the corner behind the wheel of her muscle car. He was well aware that the School of Foreign Service was on the other side of campus and that Albright would be walking farther in the rain from the lot than she would have from her home. The love affair between people and their cars, he thought.

It may have been her sports car, or it may have been the fact that, time permitting, she could be found courtside at every Georgetown Hoyas basketball home game, or it may have been that she regularly included many of her students at her dinner parties. But whatever the reason, from the time Albright taught her first class in the master's program, she had made an impact on her students that few professors at Georgetown or any other university could possibly envision. "She was like a pied piper," says Walsh School Dean Emeritus Peter Krough of Albright's abilities as a teacher. "The students flocked to her."

Ironically, for many reasons, it almost didn't happen that way.

Albright, who had been married only days after her graduation from Wellesley College with full honors in 1959, followed a path filled with detours en route to academia.

While giving birth to and raising three daughters, she managed to obtain her doctorate from Columbia University and do stints both as a staffer on Capitol Hill and for the Carter administration at the National Security Council. At every level she distinguished herself. Nevertheless, when she sought a position on the faculty of Georgetown University in 1982, she was received with less than open arms.

If the old adage that first impressions can be deceiving ever held true, it certainly applied to Madeleine Albright's first encounter with the powers that be at the Georgetown University School of Government. Much has been reported about the subject, the popular line being that while Albright was offered a job, she was relegated to the position of research professor and director of the Women in Foreign Service Program. It has also been reported that the sting of the rejection irked Albright for years and that it stemmed from an inherent resentment by many of the blue-blooded professors among Georgetown's faculty, mostly men, who looked down on her thin academic credentials.

In fact, Albright was snubbed by the Georgetown

School of Government, not the School of Foreign Service, as has been widely reported. And while she's the first to admit that the wholesale rejection of her qualifications came as a shock, leaving her both hurt and angered, it happened for reasons altogether different from what people think. Contrary to popular belief, the government department at Georgetown was not some insular, closed bastion of sexism that found Albright a threat. The reasons behind its rejection of Albright had far more to do with a general clash of cultures within the university community than anything else. For years Georgetown University has been one of the top academic institutions in the country, with a long and proud tradition of scholastic excellence. But to outsiders, it seems to suffer from an identity crisis. Given the fact that it is slightly less expensive than its Ivy League competitors, it has become a second-choice school for many top students who aspire to attend Harvard or Yale or lately, Brown University. From Georgetown's perspective, they make no apologies, boasting a top 1 percent level placement rate for its students with the nation's first-tier graduate and professional schools, as well as among the Fortune 500 corporations.

What's more, at least as many applicants who have the option to attend an Ivy League school choose to attend Georgetown as those who do not. The fact is that Georgetown tends to be a legacy school, with one of its real attractions being its extensive alumni network. And, as a true liberal arts institution, it tempers university-wide policies with the specific practices and procedures of its individual colleges and departments, going to great pains to respect the autonomy of each.

As one might expect, this applies to the hiring of faculty. As for the School of Government, it had a long history of bringing its new faculty members up through the ranks. "Homegrown" was the expression used to describe the system. More often than not, the school preferred its faculty candidates to be part of its own postgraduate program, and to have served as graduate assistants along the way. Most of all, no matter where they originated, Georgetown wanted its people to publish, and publish often. Unfortunately for Albright, who had a Ph.D. in political science and a certificate in Russian Studies, she had hardly published anything. Notwithstanding that, her credentials were impeccable: senior advisor to the chairman of the Senate Foreign Relations Committee and the director of Congressional Relations for the National Security advisor to the President, Zbigniew Brzezinski. But, in the eyes of those at the Georgetown School of Government, this was essentially irrelevant. Says one university official, "She could have had a Nobel Prize and it wouldn't have mattered." Albright just didn't fit the mold. Fortunately, for her and Georgetown University, she was exactly what the School of Foreign Service was looking for.

Albright was hired in 1982 as part of the Walsh School's interdisciplinary faculty, by Executive Dean Alan Goodman. Goodman, who was also the person who developed the Women in Foreign Service Program, which Albright headed, was impressed by Albright's perfect blend of practitioner and academic. By definition, any school of foreign service requires that its faculty offer the combination of practical experience and academic capabilities. "She was perfect for us," says Peter Krough, who had known

Albright since her undergraduate days at Wellesley in the late 1950s. "She had some policy experience, some academic background, and had been circulating in the diplomatic community for years. Unfortunately for the School of Government, they did not see in Madeleine what we saw in Madeleine. They could have benefited greatly from her insights, her experiences, the world that she occupied. But they were not prepared to ask her to join their faculty as a first-class citizen."

By all accounts, in the classroom, Professor Albright was a hard act to follow. One former student put it this way, "She was outgoing, engaged, and enthusiastic. And she easily communicated that enthusiasm to her students, which made a complicated subject much easier to understand. Professor Albright was a magnet." When it comes to Albright's uncanny ability to connect with young people, both Goodman and Krough marvel. In addition to the seminar on Women in Foreign Service, Albright was asked to teach the most difficult course in the department. "It was the mid-eighties, and given her Ph.D. in political science from Columbia and background in comparative governments, we asked Madeleine to teach a course in modern comparative foreign governments," begins Krough. "But try to remember the time frame. No sooner had she begun teaching the course, than glasnost burst on the scene."

Despite the fact that Albright was diligent in her lesson plans, with the early effects of glasnost and perestroika making an impact throughout Eastern Europe and elsewhere, she never could be certain from day to day whether or not her lecture was fully accurate on the day it was given. Many tell the story of seeing Albright walking across the Georgetown campus to a lecture hall at the campus Cultural Center, with textbooks and lesson plan under one arm, holding a folder full of the morning's latest press clippings from the national and international dailies in the other. It became part of her routine to review them the morning of every lecture to make a last-minute determination of the latest status of the particular government on which she might be lecturing. With the course coming apart as she was teaching it, Albright's challenge became that of trying to hit a moving target. "But despite the irritation of the challenge, never knowing whether a student might have spotted something on a morning newscast or overheard the latest parliamentary collapse via the car radio on the way to class that day that she might have missed, Madeleine held it together," says a colleague.

To hear Krough tell it, holding it together is something of an understatement. "She had to lecture two or three times a week to large groups of students, forge a relationship with them, maintain her credibility, fully aware that in the volatile global climate of the time some breaking development could change the face of the map overnight, not to mention the answers to questions on her exams." But despite all this, says Krough, "in every dimension of her performance at Georgetown, Madeleine was excellent." During Albright's eleven-year tenure on the faculty—she stayed until she was tapped for the UN post in 1993—she was the recipient of numerous awards and accolades, including being elected Teacher of the Year at Georgetown four times in a row. Says a faculty member, "It was really unheard of. Normally it takes a while to get established here, but not Madeleine. She established herself the day she arrived."

Many sources attest that the impact of Albright's presence at Georgetown was not limited to her students. Not long after arriving, Albright forged fast and lasting relationships with her colleagues, particularly Dean Goodman. For a number of reasons, including the fact that her course was located administratively in the Masters Program in the School of Foreign Service, as well as the fact that they shared adjacent offices on the third floor of the Cultural Center, the two developed a close professional relationship and personal friendship, and participated in many projects together. Among these included weekly "Voice of America" interviews, in which the two exchanged views on the government-sponsored news program on a variety of issues, including disarmament, Iran-Contra, humanitarian aid to Ethiopia, human rights in China, the emergent democracy movement in Poland, and the Gulf War. It was during these interviews, as well as serving as a coanchor on Peter Krough's respected "Great Decisions" public affairs program on Public Broadcasting, that she honed her media skills. In this setting she learned to pare down the long-winded, meticulously detailed answers to which academics are prone, into tight, manageable sound bites.

Albright also played a key role in Georgetown's cutting-edge Leadership Seminar, patterned after Henry Kissinger's Harvard program, in which representatives from each of the university's schools and departments, along with another seventy-five or so government officials, lawyers, bankers, journalists, and military officers from all over the world were invited to Georgetown for a week packed with sessions attended by heavyweights from the State Department, the Pentagon, and foreign capitals. Albright never missed a minute of it and never forgot a name. Designed to foster a scholarly discourse on many of the vital issues of the day, the Leadership Seminar was headed by a longtime friend of Albright's, Gail Griffith, who after her divorce in the early 1980s, lived for a time at the Albright home. "Even though she had just gone through a similar experience, she opened her home to me, extending every generosity. That was just the kind of person she was," said Griffith.

So successful was the seminar that it continued in one incarnation or another for several years with the highlight being a reunion of the group in Israel in 1988. Attending were Albright, Goodman, Krough, and Griffith, among others. Although there were any number of major geopolitical imperatives facing the international community at the time, the group still found time to do some sight-seeing. As Krough put it, "I've known Madeleine for over forty years and have been pretty much all over the world with her, Europe, Russia, Argentina, the West Bank. And, no matter what kind of a project we were working on, she always seems to enjoy herself. She always seems to find a way to soak up a little of the local color and squeeze in some fun." During this particular reunion, she and her troupe managed to do that literally.

It seems one hot, sunny day, after the seminar broke up, Albright and several others paid a visit to Masada, site of the historic fortress in which dozens of Jewish soldiers trapped by a legion of the Roman army took their own lives rather than surrender to the enemy. The fortress itself is located at the base of a large mountain overlooking the Dead Sea. So, after taking in Masada, Albright, who would have been fifty years old at the time, decided that they as a group just had to climb the mountain. This despite the fact that it was over one hundred degrees in the hot desert sun and that none of them were really dressed for it. Still they pressed on. "Madeleine is just a go-for-it person," says Krough. "She believes that you only go around once and you have to grab what life offers you when it offers it."

For hours the group made the slow trek up the steep peak, reaching the summit by midday and taking at least another hour to make their descent. By then Albright and the group were hot, tired, and thirsty. Unfortunately, despite the fact that Masada is a major tourist attraction, with vendors selling overpriced T-shirts that read "I climbed Masada and lived to tell about it," there is little in the way of refreshments or a place to take refuge from the sun. This posed a dilemma of sorts as Albright's group was virtually baking in the heat and faced at least an hour's drive back to Tel Aviv.

"I'd kill for a diet Coke about now," said Albright.

"Whose idea was it to climb that stupid mountain, anyway?" joked one of the group.

"It was my stupid idea, thank you very much," she responded.

"Okay, you got us in this, now you get us out of it," came the response.

Albright was stymied, but only temporarily. It had been a great day, Masada was magnificent and very moving. The climb had been exhilarating and the camaraderie with her friends first rate. Now, if she could only find a way for them to cool off before they passed out from heatstroke. And then the solution appeared right before her eyes, literally. The Dead Sea. Not exactly the Riviera or the pool at the Beverly Wilshire, but as hot as they were, it suited their purposes just fine. So, with just the right amount of encouragement from Albright and Krough, this highly sophisticated group of American intellectuals, collectively embodying some of the top foreign policy talent in the country, all walked the hundred or so feet to the shore of the body of water and plunged headfirst into the Dead Sea for a desperately needed afternoon swim. As Krough tells it, "We didn't stop to think about whether we were allowed to swim in the Dead Sea or not, whether or not it was polluted or safe. We just knew we wanted to go swimming." When asked whether or not the group went in with clothes on or skinny-dipped, Krough burst into laughter, "Of course we had our clothes on. There were Israeli soldiers all over the place. With guns."

Of course there were many other special moments between Albright and her newfound family in the School of Foreign Service—the dinner parties, the trips, the academic honors. For several years in a row she hosted the faculty fall orientation retreat at her 370-acre horse farm in the Virginia countryside. Normally the retreat was treated as strictly a working session by faculty members who used it to preview the upcoming school year. But during the period Albright hosted it, it became kind of a tame version of spring break for the faculty. "Everyone arrived early and everyone stayed late," says one colleague. Krough reminisces about the first time they drove there with his colleagues, speculating that it was near Middleburg or some other burg in Virginia's high-end countryside. "But when we arrived, what we found was this beautiful, huge, tract of land and this rustic and decidedly simple farmhouse. Like everything else about Madeleine, it was comfortable. Normal and nice."

Shortly after Albright was appointed ambassador to the United Nations, President Clinton, recognizing the connection between the Walsh School and the inhabitants of Embassy Row, chose the occasion of January 18, 1993, to introduce himself to the diplomatic community. In the early morning at Georgetown, the President planned his speech. With virtually every foreign ambassador to the United States, along with the upper tier of the State Department, and the Walsh School faculty gathered in the courtyard of the oldest building on campus, Gaston Church, President Clinton—Albright seated right behind him—said hello to the rest of the world from the portico of the old church. After the President-elect's speech, which was exceptionally well received according to several sources, the affair was moved to the Cultural Center for a short reception and receiving line. Given the timing of the event—in only a couple of hours the President-elect was to begin the traditional weeklong series of inaugural events—the Secret Service, which was still adjusting to the new chief executive, was obsessive about keeping him on schedule. Unfortunately, they had no way of knowing that the

President and the new ambassador to the UN were about to participate in the slowest receiving line in modern presidential history. He was on Madeleine Albright's turf, these were her people. Certainly they had all come out and braved the freezing temperatures to hear the new President speak, but they had also come out to wish Albright well. That truly was the day that Clinton-Time—Washington-speak for the fact that this White House almost never stays on schedule—was born. The receiving line was scheduled to begin at 9:45 A.M. and last forty-five minutes to allow the roughly two hundred guests to the reception to shake the President's hand and have a photo op. Finally, at 12:05 P.M. the last guest had passed through the line. To hear the White House advance team tell it, almost every single guest felt compelled to hold up the line, hugging and kissing Albright, bestowing congratulations on her, shaking the President-elect's hand, posing for the photo and then with some, going back to hug her one more time. Said one Secret Service veteran, "I've been with this detail almost twenty years and I've never seen anybody hugged and kissed so much in my life." Said another, "It's gonna be a long four years."

After the reception, Albright and selected guests retired to the home of Peter Krough, who also happens to be her neighbor, where he held a private luncheon in her honor. The guest list reading like a who's who of the Washington power scene, included Pamela Harriman, former UN envoys Donald McHenry, Jeane Kirkpatrick, Manatt, Kelly and Senators Barbara Mikulski and Patrick Leahy. A number of guests describe how Albright sat beaming at the head of the table, and while relishing the moment, was a little embarrassed by the adulation. Krough, for his part, sensed this and modified his toast accordingly. After spending almost ten minutes extolling Albright's virtues, he recalled a timeless saying by Adlai Stevenson—an idol of Albright's—on the subject of flattery.

"Stevenson," said Krough, "was a true lover of flattery. In fact, with all due respect to President Clinton, Stevenson had been quoted as saying 'Flattery is fine, as long as you don't inhale!'" As many around the table turned red at the reference, they were aware nonetheless, that today, Albright loved being the center of attention, yet she always remained grounded, down to earth. She would be the last person to ever inhale the smell of her newfound success and run the risk of becoming intoxicated with power. No matter what one said, she just keeps on being Madeleine.

As Dean Alan Goodman said of the woman he once hired as she rose to prominence, knowing that her appointment made her departure certain, "She comes to the job from central casting. She has done it all: raised a family of three brilliant daughters; worked for two brilliant minds, Brzezinski and Muskie; earned a doctorate degree in this field; worked in three political campaigns. She is going to be someone who is credible selling foreign policy to soccer moms as well as Middle Eastern potentates and Bosnian warlords."

The sheer value of the high regard which Albright's university colleagues have for her is simply beyond measure. Both in an academic setting and in the diplomatic community generally, the esteem of her peers speaks volumes to Albright's intellect and charm. And as important as this was in defining her reputation as the foreign policy guru of the Democratic Party, far more compelling in the long run was her relationship with her students.

As Goodman, Krough, and several other colleagues can verify, the relationship between Dr. Albright and her students was akin to that of a rock star and her fans. Adoring, loyal, and filled with boundless enthusiasm for learning, most of her students often found that the hardest part of her Comparative Government course wasn't the final exam, but saying good-bye. And over time, many of them would learn to their surprise, with Madeleine Albright, there really was no such thing as good-bye. Rather, with the vast majority of her students, it was more of a case of *au revoir*.

The math speaks for itself. During her eleven years at Georgetown, Albright lectured on Comparative Government to roughly one hundred students a semester, three times a week. That worked out to 1,200 direct contacts per month. More precisely, not counting one-on-one student conferences, over an eleven-year period Albright delivered 118,800 lectures to 2,200 future diplomats, policy wonks, academics, congressional aides, foreign agents, and investment bankers. Today, it is almost impossible to attend a meeting with an international component at the United Nations, any think tank, major university, or on Capitol Hill without running into someone who was taught by Madeleine Albright. In short, she built the Ultimate Farm Team of decision makers in Washington, New York, and major capitals throughout the world. Decision makers with whom she had a long-standing personal connection. And while it goes without saying that there is no way that Albright could have foreseen the growth of such a network, the advantage it offers her is undeniable. Washington is known as a place in which familiarity often breeds contempt, but in Albright's case it has had the opposite effect—deep, abiding respect born out of gratitude and admiration.

To any number of observers, it would seem that Albright had led a charmed life. Born the child of a prominent, up-and-coming diplomat, attending some of the best schools both Europe and this country had to offer, it might seem that Albright's career path was paved for her well before she ever graduated from college. However, although Madeleine Albright's accomplishments to date are beyond compare, that she began the process well into her thirties and succeeded in the endeavor is truly incredible.

In a way it started on the day of her graduation from Wellesley, a prestigious women's college, when her class's graduation speaker announced that, despite the honors she had earned, it would be her role in life to "raise the next generation of educated citizens." This came as quite a blow to Madeleine Korbel, who as an undergraduate studied her twin passions of journalism and politics, graduating magna cum laude. She edited the school newspaper and participated in a host of campus activities. And despite the fact that she was residing on an overwhelmingly Republican campus, she was an early supporter of Adlai Stevenson. Then, only three days after graduation, she married the scion of one of America's wealthiest families, publishing heir Joseph Medill Albright. The year was 1959, and no sooner had Joe decided to move to Chicago to take a position with the *Sun-Times* than Albright's career as a journalist came summarily to an end. "There was no way anybody in town would hire a woman whose husband worked for a competitor," said Joe's editor. "You have an obligation to your husband to find another line of work," she was told by others in the industry.

This began a rather long period of over twenty years, in which Madeleine Albright's destiny was not her own. This, in and of itself, is not all that surprising for a woman of that era. What is surprising is that for over two decades Albright fought little by little, in every way she could, to regain control of her life. Beginning with the move to Chicago, the first of several career-driven relocations in years to come at husband Joe's behest, Albright was a virtual professional nomad, unable to put down roots or build a professional network. The fact that she gave birth to three daughters during that period was less than helpful.

Quite frankly, though, not everyone was altogether sympathetic to her dilemma. After all, despite the fact that her career was subordinated, she was neverthless married to an attractive, wealthy man, with whom she had built a family. The Albrights lived well, traveled extensively, rarely wanted for anything. So what was the problem, some of her contemporaries wondered?

The problem, put simply, was that she, like so many

women of that era, was stuck, relegated to second-class status. Couple this with a profoundly optimistic view of life's potential born out of the inspiration of her father, who extracted his family from the mantle of totalitarian dictatorships twice, immigrating to this country to build a new life—and the inevitable conclusion for Albright was that she needed to do more simply because she had the innate capability to do more. To her, there wasn't really any question of what she had to do. She was determined. She would never give up.

With her husband putting in long hours at *Newsday*, Albright assumed most of the parental responsibilities raising their three daughters Alice, Anne, and Katharine, yet still managed to enroll in a graduate program at Columbia University where she studied under future boss Zbigniew Brzezinski. In 1968 she earned her certificate in Russian Studies. Things were beginning to look up as Albright attempted to redirect her career in the realm of foreign relations until Joe Albright dropped yet another bomb on her: he had been offered a promotion to head *Newsday*'s Washington news bureau and had accepted. The family was moving to D.C. in two weeks.

So for the third time in eight years, Madeleine Albright's life, career, and world had been uprooted by the geographical imperatives of her husband's career. For the third time she had seen all her hard work to develop a local network of relationships in her field effectively muted by distance. She was about to enter the Ph.D. program at Columbia. Now what?

After considering any number of options, Albright

knew she had just come too far to give up. Many who know her say that she simply is not capable of quitting. So she made the decision to pursue her doctorate anyway, communicating with her faculty advisor via phone and mail, making an occasional trip to New York for a face-to-face consultation. Rising every morning at 4:30 A.M. Albright put her nose to the grindstone, to study and to write, knowing that if she ever wanted to make it outside the comfortable environs of marriage, she could not let up. Calling her dissertation the hardest thing she ever did, Albright wrote on the role of the Czech press in the 1968 Prague Spring. Based on documents and numerous interviews with Czech dissidents, the thesis examines the role of the fourth estate in the downfall of the old regime. Over the years Albright has kept in close touch with many of the former dissidents, including, of course, Václav Havel. And even though Albright took on numerous other projects during that time, including fund-raising for a prestigious Washington-area private school and the 1972 Muskie presidential campaign, she finally became Dr. Madeleine Albright in 1976, when she was awarded her Ph.D. from Columbia.

For most people, the dogged determination necessary to resurrect one's career after a major setback often carries with it a cost. Generally one's health, friendships, or relationships with one's own family suffer in the process. But in Albright's situation this was apparently not the case. Close friends attest that despite the fact that she is much thinner than she photographs, she is very conscious of the fat content of what she eats. Other than an occasional glass of wine, she hardly drinks alcohol. "If it isn't healthy, Madeleine won't put it in her mouth," says one friend. Albright herself has joked about the buffet- and banquet-laden tour of duty at the United Nations, saying that unlike other UN envoys, "I did not come here just to eat for my country." Accordingly, she is the picture of health, despite the upheavals in her life.

As for friendships, much of the aforementioned speaks to that. But what is truly fascinating is that Albright, while struggling to fulfill her education, was proud of being a mom first. According to daughter Anne, a lawyer specializing in family practice in Rockville, Maryland, just outside of Washington, "My sisters and I never felt that our mother didn't have enough time for us. She's always done the ordinary things that mothers do: getting us up in the mornings and ready for school, helping us with our homework. We used to do our homework together: she was finishing her Ph.D. and we were in grade school. On Fridays she would do the grocery shopping while my sisters and I were horseback riding or taking ballet classes or guitar lessons. She was just the coolest mom. We had a wonderful family life."

As Dean Goodman said, Madeleine Albright chose to do it all. And while the road to her success contained far more curves and was much rockier than most could have imagined, it is her uncanny ability to turn setbacks into opportunity that sets her apart. It took her over fifteen years to redefine herself professionally, yet she never gave up, knowing that if she persevered she would someday carve out a niche of her own in the world. By her own admission she has succeeded beyond her wildest dreams. But perhaps the most intriguing element of her climb back is that the best of Madeleine Albright is still yet to come.

Last spring, former President Gerald Ford called Albright the "Tiger Woods of foreign policy." While the analogy is flattering it is somewhat inaccurate. Tiger Woods is an enormously talented twenty-one-year-old who shattered every barrier and broke every record in winning his first Major, and at his age, cannot have any idea about how good he will someday be. For Madeleine Albright it took thirty years to win the equivalent of her first Major, and as the ultimate student of the possible, she is well aware of how good she is right now and must be in the future.

4

THE UNDIPLOMATIC DIPLOMAT

Ambassador Albright's Days

at the United Nations

There is little doubt that Albright's arrival at Foggy Bottom promised to shake up the staid old agency. But no matter what surprises she had in store for her colleagues in the diplomatic corps, she would have to go a long way to outdo her performance as this country's Special Representative to the United Nations. When she accepted President-elect Clinton's nomination in the weeks following the Democratic victory, the position of UN ambassador had a very specific and somewhat limited portfolio. By the time Madeleine Albright had finished her first year in office, she had so completely transformed and redefined the position that substantive comparison to her predecessors was simply a waste of time.

From the moment the President introduced her as his UN envoy in December 1992, Albright made it clear how much she treasured the opportunity. Recalling her own refugee experience, she used the press conference to communicate just how personal the appointment was to her. "As a result of the generous spirit of the American people, our family had the privilege of growing up as free Americans," she told *The Washington Post.* "You can therefore understand how proud I will be to sit at the United Nations behind the nameplate that says UNITED STATES OF AMERICA."

Madeleine Albright's dutiful, almost reverential view of her responsibility as America's UN ambassador carried forth to her confirmation hearings before the Senate Foreign Relations Committee. And while the Democrats still controlled the committee back in 1993, the White House had told their nominee to prepare for the worst, that Republican Senator Jesse Helms simply hated the United Nations as an institution and would be out for blood. Advisors relayed stories of how the senior senator from North Carolina regularly roughed up previous envoys such as Vernon Waters and Thomas Pickering, despite the fact that both were serving Republican presidents. Despite the warnings, Ambassador-designate Albright was unfazed. "With me, what you see is what you get," she told close friend and mentor Edmund Muskie, the legendary senator and former secretary of state. "If the senators on the committee don't like what I have to say, then they don't like it."

President Clinton watches Madeleine Albright being sworn in as the new U.S. Secretary of State, the first woman to hold this office. AGENCE FRANCE PRESSE/CORBIS-BETTMANN

Madeleine Albright with Daw Aung San Suu Kyi, the political activist and winner of the Nobel Peace Prize.
AGENCE FRANCE PRESSE/CORBIS-BETTMANN

Secretary of State Albright meets with French Premier Alain Juppé. AGENCE FRANCE PRESSE/CORBIS-BETTMANN

Madeleine Albright shakes hands with Fumio Kyuka, Japan's defense chief. AGENCE FRANCE PRESSE/CORBIS-BETTMANN

Shinji Sato, Minister for International Trade and Industry, greets Madeleine Albright. AGENCE FRANCE PRESSE/CORBIS-BETTMANN

Hillary Clinton and Madeleine Albright.
AGENCE FRANCE PRESSE/CORBIS-BETTMANN

Madeleine Albright meets at the State Department with Vesna Pesic (right), *Vuk Draskovic, and Zoran Djindjic* (left), *members of the Serb opposition.* AGENCE FRANCE PRESSE/CORBIS-BETTMANN

Substituting for an ailing President Clinton, Madeleine Albright throws out the first pitch before the Royals-Orioles opening-day baseball game. AGENCE FRANCE PRESSE/CORBIS-BETTMANN

President Clinton and Secretary of State Albright with French counterparts, President Jacques Chirac (right) *and Foreign Minister Hervé de Charette* (center).

President-elect Clinton and Vice President–elect Gore with Albright and other appointees, December 1992.

Secretary of State Warren Christopher testifies before the Senate as Secretary of State–designate Madeleine Albright watches during her confirmation hearings.

Madeleine Albright with Nasir Jabucar in his souvenir shop during her 1996 visit to war-torn Sarajevo.
AGENCE FRANCE PRESSE/CORBIS-BETTMANN

Secretary of State Albright speaking at a State Department press conference. AGENCE FRANCE PRESSE/CORBIS-BETTMANN

On January 21, 1993, the Senate Foreign Relations Committee convened to listen to what Madeleine Albright had to say.

They liked it.

Dressed in a teal Chanel suit and glowing brighter than the barrage of camera flashes that exploded at her when she began to speak, Albright made her feelings known. "History will record that the end of the Cold War has marked a new beginning for the United Nations. I am firmly convinced that, today, we are witnessing the best chance for fulfilling the United Nation's original mission." As the entire panel was transfixed by her every word, she reminded the committee that the mission statement of the UN Charter calls upon the peoples of the United Nations to "save succeeding generations from the scourge of war, to reaffirm faith in fundamental human rights, to establish conditions under which justice and respect for international law can be maintained, and to promote social progress and better standards of life in larger freedom. . . . We not only need to fulfill their dreams but also to make this international organization face the challenges of the next century," she proclaimed before a packed hearing room. "If we do not act today, we may not have another chance."

As Albright spoke, the reactions of those in the ornate chamber were telling. Veteran Foreign Relations panel member and friend Patrick Leahy beamed with pride, doing his best to contain his enthusiasm and evince a demeanor appropriate for the number two ranking member of the committee. Then-Chairman Claiborne Pell made no such attempt, grinning openly and often, nodding, almost as if he was rooting the nominee on. But the most subtle yet compelling reaction was that of Senator Jesse Helms who, as Albright's opening statement began, was conspicuously studying a list of questions prepared by his own staff, numbering seventy-five pages. Word had it that the list was so comprehensive, and some say so confrontational, that Helms had his aides working well past two in the morning in an attempt to include any and every possible query as to weaknesses in American foreign policy and the efficacy of the United Nations.

And then something unexpected occurred. Roughly two minutes into Albright's prepared statement, the senator, who had yet to make eye contact with the nominee, suddenly stopped reading and looked up through his half-rim glasses. The line that got the Senator's attention was Albright's rather hawkish declaration that as UN ambassador, she would "never advocate giving up sovereignty of the American people in an area where it was in our national interest." As the nominee read on, Senator Helms— a crusty gentleman, standing about six feet two inches tall and a not so svelte two hundred and forty pounds, known for his dour suits, impeccably starched shirts, and expensive neckwear—began to take notice. Seated before him was not some far-out, left-wing proponent of conciliation, but rather, a tough, passionate, anti-Communist, unashamed of her Munich mind-set.

The fact that Albright shared the view of a significant bloc of senators soon became clear, as she testified that, "US leadership in world politics and in multilateral organizations is a fundamental tenet of the Clinton administration." It was at that very moment that Jesse Helms, without taking his eyes off the ambassador-designate, ever so discreetly handed his seventy-five-page interrogatories to an aide seated nearby. The aide, who hadn't been to sleep for forty-eight hours, was stunned.

Minutes passed, with the senator listening attentively to her every word. When she concluded her opening statement, Chairman Pell opened the floor to questions. For roughly two hours, several Democratic senators tossed Albright nothing but softballs, making it so easy that Senator Leahy chimed in, asking his old friend to elaborate here and there, just to lend a little credibility to the Democratic line of questioning. Late that afternoon, when it was the Republicans' turn, Senator Helms led off. But, unlike other members of the panel, he embarked on his line of interrogation with no prepared text or line of questioning.

The media, which had been anticipating a combative exchange between Albright and Helms for most of the morning, was sadly disappointed. While Helms took his shots at the United Nations, he seemed to go out of his way to be solicitous of Albright. Later senior Senate aides admitted that it was an emotional experience for the senator, who realized in the midst of her opening statement that Madeleine Albright was not only the first foreign-born American to be nominated as UN ambassador, but the first refugee. After the first day of hearings, the gravelly voiced Helms would confide to an old friend that "Albright understands the world like a refugee, a multilingual, multicultural warrior for human rights and democratic principles."

Despite the fact that many of the Republicans were still in shock over Bill Clinton's election victory two months earlier, the Senate unanimously confirmed Madeleine Albright on January 27, 1993. And while most assumed that they were voting to confirm her as the United States Permanent Representative to the United Nations, they, in fact, were getting much more than they bargained for. Unlike his predecessor, George Bush, President Clinton was not only intent on restoring the position of UN envoy to cabinet level, but also on bestowing the rank of ambassador extraordinary and plenipotentiary on Albright. As if that wasn't enough to give the longtime Democratic foreign policy maven clout within his administration, Clinton appointed her as a full member of the National Security Council. As such, she was expected to attend a biweekly principals' meeting that included herself, the Director of Intelligence, the Secretaries of State and Defense, and the National Security Advisor. By the time she presented her credentials to the United Nations General Assembly on February 1, 1993, she was well positioned, in the opinion of respected foreign affairs reporter Richard Chesnoff, to wield "power and influence unprecedented for an American envoy to the UN."

During the first weeks of her tenure at the UN, Ambassador Albright underwent a period of adjustment that can only be described as a study in chaos management. Given her multiple roles in the new administration, Albright was expected not only to perform her ambassadorial duties on the floor of the General Assembly, but attend regularly scheduled cabinet and National Security Council meetings.

Combining this with the aforementioned principals' meetings, as well as impromptu skull sessions convened at the President's discretion, made for the mother of all scheduling nightmares for Albright and her staff. She was a regular on the La Guardia–National Airport shuttle between New York and Washington, often traveling between the two cities as many as five times a week, generally catching the 6:45 A.M. flight. As grueling as this schedule may have seemed, Ambassador Albright, relentless in her commitment, was as guilty as anybody in overloading her own schedule. Longtime aide Rubin has gone on record as saying that it was not unusual for his boss to demand a pre-dawn briefing on the airport tarmac, one of two daily briefings that were "an orthodox ritual for her." Another senior intelligence aide added, "We were told, 'Whatever you do, don't mess with Madeleine's schedule.'"

Additionally, during her first few weeks as head of the American delegation, Albright went through an uncharacteristic period of difficulty adjusting to the hordes of reporters that regularly stalk the key delegates at the United Nations. The normally media savvy envoy appeared skittish with the ever-present international media camped outside the Security Council pressing her for statements concerning US positions on any number of vital international issues. Additionally, due to the fact that Albright was one of only seven female permanent residents among the 184 in the assembly, her gender was the focus of more than one article. More than once, she confessed her exasperation with journalists who seemed hell-bent on writing about her appearance as if what color dress she was wearing played a pivotal role in a negotiation. In one memorable exchange, during one of the countless eat-and-greet buffets held at the Assembly, Albright spotted a reporter from a Rome weekly who had written a three-page feature critiquing her dowdy ensemble a month earlier. With neither Albright nor her staff having made any attempt to conceal their irritation with the article, the author of the piece actually seemed to enjoy his newfound foray into controversy.

About that time, the reporter, somewhat emboldened by the notoriety, started to approach Albright. But by the time he got near the ambassador, her icy stare had riveted him, stopping the reporter dead in his tracks. "If I wear a red suit and you say that I look like a fat little red ball, then that's your problem," she stated forcefully as the scribe stood frozen, somewhat embarrassed. As a European he wasn't used to women speaking to men in that fashion, especially not at the United Nations. Later that night, via phone to Los Angeles, Albright would vent to confidante Streisand, who did her best to console her, sensing that her close friend was exposing a rarely seen vulnerable side. "When I work, I really work. I rub my eyes and my makeup comes off. So I've given up worrying about my appearance," said the ambassador.

Streisand, who perhaps better than anyone understands the constant media attention surrounding Albright, has been quite vocal about their friendship. "You know, you meet certain people and you have a rapport or you don't. You share the same kind of feelings about life and politics and whatever. We talk about everything." They also share the common bond of being extremely powerful women in a world dominated by men. Putting this in perspective, Streisand says of herself and Albright, "We're not toughies. And yet we are tough in some ways. I mean we're multi-faceted. We're little girls at moments, we're teenagers and we're grown-ups. And we'd like to be accepted for all those qualities. And the rare person sees through the powerful position and sees you as a woman."

And while to some, this may make the ambassador seem a little hypersensitive on this issue, she has any number of defenders who are quick to point out the extreme sexism that permeates virtually every aspect of the United Nations. One unlikely defender is National Security Advisor Anthony Lake, who is not shy about saying, "If her name was Mike, or Mark, or Max instead of Madeleine, neither her gender nor her mode of dress would even come into play."

Fortunately, as time passed, Albright made the adjustment, eventually becoming the de facto talk-show host for the Clinton administration on such thorny issues as Somalia, the war in Bosnia-Herzegovina, and human rights in China.

In short order, Albright embraced her new post as a multimedia bully pulpit, wasting no time in enunciating the United States's position on a multitude of issues. Included among her more memorable sound bites was her response when asked by Senator Helms to address the contentious issue of the ever-bloated UN budget. Without blinking an eye, Albright responded, "The UN bureaucracy has grown to elephantine proportions. Now that the Cold War is over, we are asking that elephant to do gymnastics." When asked to differentiate between American trade policy with the People's Republic of China versus Castro's Cuba, the ambassador was characteristically blunt, "We do not have a cookie-cutter approach to policy. China is a world power. . . . Cuba is an embarrassment to the Western world." But more than anything, Madeleine Albright followed a unique credo that continues to define her tenure as the American emissary. As she often says to top aide Rubin, "When we weigh in on an issue publicly, we weigh in all the way."

Due in part to the post-Cold War environment in which she served, Albright stylistically reinvented the portfolio of UN Ambassador. For more than three decades, with the United Nations paralyzed by superpower-driven gridlock, American emissaries were little more than talking heads, regal mouthpieces seeking to communicate the US point of view in the hope of expanding American influence. The styles of the many who preceded Albright have largely been a function of the goals of the administration in which they served. Adlai Stevenson, a cerebral and enormously idealistic man, got the appointment because members of the cabinet saw him as a constant source of competition in the foreign policy arena and wanted him out of town. People often forget that among the many posts in which he served, George Bush did a stint as the American envoy to the UN. Not surprisingly, he distinguished himself there not by any level of significant accomplishment, but by being dubbed the Mr. Congeniality of the General Assembly. More exciting was Andrew Young, charming and outspoken, who spent much of his tenure globe-trotting to never-before-visited foreign capitals, particularly in Africa. But if there was one Permanent Representative whose style Albright seems to most emulate, it would be that of Nixon-Ford envoy, Daniel Patrick Moynihan, now a United States senator. Moynihan's blunt-spoken, in-your-face style appealed to the young Madeleine Albright, then a Columbia graduate student who admired his dignified refusal to be intimidated by a UN Security Council that was, at the time, clearly in the camp of the Soviet Union, a mere conduit for anti-American and anti-Israeli sentiment. Indeed, on the floor of the General Assembly, the Moynihan comparisons were frequent, whether in a debate with an Iraqi diplomat making the ludicrous charge that American-backed economic sanctions against the Saddam Hussein government were designed to "kill Iraqi children," or playing tough with a North Korean delegate over his government's refusal to allow inspectors from the International Atomic Energy Agency to conduct inspections of its plutonium processing plants.

But for all the tough talk and legendary tête-à-têtes which seem to define Madeleine Albright, part of the personal style she brought to the post as US delegate was, by all accounts, desperately needed in the staid old body—a sense of humor. Rather than decorate her office in the traditional mode favored by many of her colleagues, Ambassador Albright's inner sanctum includes a bust of longtime hero Adlai Stevenson adorned with a blue UN hard hat and a green beret. Nearby is an autographed Harlem Globetrotters basketball. By all accounts though, her favorite is the broom she keeps behind her desk, a gift from a Middle Eastern delegate who found her demeanor so offensive that he called her a cruel witch, suggesting that she ride it back to Washington on it.

Moreover, Albright's edgy view of what is funny goes beyond the confines of her office. She was the first to admit that being the only woman on the fifteen-member UN Security Council took a little getting used to. Nevertheless, she took great pains to surprise the other ambassadors on Valentine's Day by giving them each a red bag of candy and cookies. And while Albright certainly had no way of knowing this, at least three delegates on the Security Council had never seen a valentine and had no idea how to interpret the gesture. One ambassador, in fact, was so unnerved by the joke that he immediately consulted his delegation's protocol officer for a clarification of his country's official position concerning the Valentine Affair. As for Albright, who had always told daughter Anne, a Washington lawyer, that "there is nothing wrong with being feminine," she found the whole thing to be a hoot. "Only at the UN," she would later tell friends.

Given the unprecedented post-Cold War climate in which Albright served, there is a great temptation for Western diplomats to put form over substance. After all, with the Soviet Union no more, it takes little strong-arming for the United States to achieve its goals on a day-to-day basis. The Russian Republic won't challenge American objectives so long as it is left alone in the countries that were once part of the USSR or the Eastern Bloc; permanent Security Council member China is unlikely to veto any resolution that does not directly affect its own security. Hence, during

Albright's tenure as envoy, there was every reason to pursue a foreign policy course that followed the path of least resistance, to seek modest goals in exchange for institutional harmony. But, as anyone who knows her will attest, Madeleine Albright cares little for institutional harmony, particularly when innocent lives are at stake in countless trouble spots around the globe.

Indeed, Albright singlehandedly transformed her post from mere messenger to chief architect and articulator of American foreign policy. While many pundits cautioned that 1993 was not the time for the United States to pursue an ambitious foreign policy agenda, UN Ambassador Albright was recommending precisely the opposite to her boss.

With Secretary of State Warren Christopher focusing much of his energies on the Middle East, Ambassador Albright saw an opening and took it. Using her combined portfolios of ambassador and NSC member, she inspected peacekeeping operations and UN initiatives in more than two dozen countries, including the former Yugoslavian republics of Bosnia, Croatia, and Slovenia; the former Soviet republics of Moldova, Armenia, and Azerbaijan; the African nations of Somalia, Ethiopia, Mozambique, and the Sudan; Cambodia, in Asia; in Central America, El Salvador; and in the Caribbean, Haiti. Along the way, Ambassador Albright cultivated a virtual credit line of goodwill with heads of states who could never have, in any other era than Albright's, expected a visit from a US envoy of her rank. "Getting to meet presidents and prime ministers is the best part of my job," she says.

Albright played an unprecedented role for a UN envoy, that of senior foreign policy strategist during the first term of the Clinton administration. In tandem with the other key members of the foreign policy team—Christopher, Defense Secretary William Perry, National Security Advisor Anthony Lake, and his deputy Sandy Berger, she not only bore the responsibility of articulating and selling the administration's position, but was as responsible as anyone for creating it. A classic example of this was the much-debated, American-led invasion of Haiti. In July of 1994, a state department memo was expressly clear in its conclusion, stating that it would be folly to seek a UN Security Council Resolution in support of military intervention. Both Secretaries Christopher and Perry concurred. But Ambassador Albright, herself a strong supporter of the invasion to put down the military junta, and well aware of the President's strong desire to see democracy restored to the island republic, opted to bypass the White House decision-making apparatus and went directly to the Commander in Chief.

There she made her request. "If you give me the go-ahead, I think I can get the votes." President Clinton, ever a believer in Albright's ability to back up what she said, decided to give it a shot.

Albright immediately went to work. Utilizing a high-risk, unorthodox strategy that focused not on the five permanent members of the Security Council—besides the United States, they include Britain, France, China, and the Russian Republic—each of whom have automatic veto power over any resolution, she instead tried to mobilize support among the ten other rotating members. This course carried with it a very real chance of backfiring, and the ambassador knew it, fully aware that she had some detractors who deeply resented her presence on the Council—with at least one delegate having not so affectionately dubbed her the queen of mean.

Nevertheless, Albright, a political deal-maker by instinct, was certain that several members of the Security Council would fondly remember her official trips to their homelands, not to mention the lavish praise she was known to laud on her diplomatic colleagues in front of their respective heads of state.

Another obstacle was time. In the business of diplomatic relations, the consensus-building component of getting a resolution written, let alone passed, is an agonizingly slow process. Even with a popular cause, position papers have to be written, translated, circulated, and, of course, discussed among senior staff. By the time a resolution gets to the Security Council, most of the big issues have been resolved. Any unresolved questions that remain generally reflect either an insurmountable impasse or the fact that a particular delegate is seeking a media forum to promote the position of his respective country.

With Security Council Resolution 940 on the status of Haiti, Albright knew that every hour of delay meant that the citizens of Port-au-Prince were in danger of being rounded up and imprisoned by the dreaded Tontons Macoutes, the much feared secret police of the Haitian military junta. What's more, every day the network news

carried live footage of boatloads of desperate Haitian refugees, fearing for their lives, attempting to sail to the coast
of Florida in makeshift vessels. On several occasions, the
reports showed the fragile boats capsizing in high seas, losing all aboard. In plain terms, she knew that democracy
had to be restored in Haiti and it had to be restored immediately. So, ever the taskmaster, Madeleine Albright,
along with her staff, burned the midnight oil fine-tuning
the resolution. Instead of circulating the draft resolution
for comments per standard procedure, the ambassador instructed an aide to set up meetings with each of the key
delegates as soon as possible. Then Albright, not the type
of person to stand on ceremony, made the rounds, resolution in hand, going directly to fellow Security Council
members' offices. As for document translation, there was
no need, as Albright herself is fluent in five languages and
was well enough versed in the native tongues of her colleagues to get the point across. By nightfall she had made
her case to every rotating member of the Security Council.
All that was necessary was to wait as each delegate con-
ferred with his country's foreign minister.

Knowing that the length of time for each delegate to get
sign-off was impossible to predict, Albright used the window of opportunity to make subtle overtures to the British
and German ambassadors, gaining their support for intervention in Haiti in short order. As for the rest, knowing
that she almost certainly had assembled a supermajority,
she waited to see what the overall reaction was before approaching them. At the UN sometimes the best strategy is
to allow certain member nations to avoid publicly an-

nouncing a position on a matter for as long as possible. For the US this is particularly true when dealing with countries in which significant pockets of anti-American sentiment are pervasive in their population.

After two days of waiting, Albright and her staff began to get anxious despite the fact that virtually everyone knew that bringing a resolution of this type to vote could take weeks. As for the White House, its patience was growing thin, demonstrated by the fact that NSC Advisor Anthony Lake's office was calling on the hour for updates. Finally, on the third day the responses began to roll in. Albright not only had her supermajority, but appeared to have garnered enough support—even getting the vote of the bewildered delegate of the Valentine Affair—to make a strong case to the permanent members if so needed. Fortunately, further strong-arming was unnecessary as every Security Council member solidly lined up behind the US, even perennial spoiler France, which often treats cooperation with the US as sacrilege.

Within hours of achieving passage of the resolution that authorized the use of military force in Haiti, Ambassador Albright, speaking before a packed UN General Assembly, issued the following warning to the leaders of the island nation's military junta. "Either you can leave voluntarily and soon, or you can leave involuntarily and soon."

In the end, UN Resolution 940 passed unanimously, and on October 15, 1994, the lawfully elected President of Haiti, Reverend Jean-Bertrand Aristide, was restored to power.

*   *   *

For Ambassador Madeleine Albright, an American envoy of unheard-of power and influence, her time at the United Nations represented a pivotal period of her life. Unlike some who represent their country's interest on the floor of the General Assembly with a single narrow point of view, often betraying a transparent agenda of self-interest, Albright the refugee is a world citizen and sees the issues confronting the international community that way. She has also been clear on the moral obligation of the United States as the "indispensable nation" to uphold its responsibility as the only democratic superpower. "Neither our history, nor our character, nor our self-interest will allow us to withdraw from the center stage of global, political, and economic life," she has said.

Toward this end, Albright sometimes thinks the United States acts as its own worst enemy. Betraying her frustration over the unwillingness of the Congress to appropriate the monies to pay the long-delinquent dues owed by the United States as a member nation of the UN (conservatively estimated at $1.2 billion), Albright went on record saying, "I do not believe I can fulfill my mission to the UN unless I am also able to persuade the American people of the importance of the mission. Yes, it costs money to help keep peace around the world. But by any measure, the most expensive peacekeeping mission is a bargain compared to the least expensive war—not just because it costs fewer dollars, but because it costs fewer lives, creating fewer orphans and refugees, and because it plants the seeds of future reconciliation, not future revenge."

During her tenure as ambassador, Albright left an indelible imprint on the UN's response to several international trouble spots. In addition to Haiti, chief among her concerns were of course such high profile undertakings as the Somalia conflict and the Bosnian civil war, as well as a number of less-publicized crises, such as the mass genocide in Rwanda and the resulting civil unrest in Burundi.

In Rwanda, the tiny, landlocked Central African nation, the horrors of civil war between the rival Hutu and Tutsi tribes and the resultant slaughter of hundreds of thousands of innocent civilians following the death of Rwanda's president in a 1994 plane crash, appalled the world community. In response, Albright, wearing both the hat of UN envoy, as well as senior administration foreign-policy architect, aggressively led the charge for expansion of UN peacekeeping forces in Rwanda and the surrounding countries of Tanzania and Zaire, while at the same time convincing the President to order a massive airlift of $150 million in relief supplies, including desperately needed food and medicine. Albright herself went to the war-ravaged country to inspect the distribution apparatus of medical supplies and foodstuffs. There, she warned the Tutsi-led government that it must adopt a policy of reconciliation with the Hutu rebels. Additionally, acting on behalf of the United Nations, Albright pressed for the release of many of the sixty thousand Hutus under arrest in Rwanda on suspicion of taking part in the 1994 massacres.

And while Albright and the United Nations were successful in brokering a short-term peace in Rwanda, the mass genocide sent thousands of desperate Rwandan refugees fleeing across the border, prompting extremist factions in nearby Burundi to seize power. For over a year the country has been teetering on the brink of civil war. While the UN Secretary General proposed the deployment of a peace-keeping force to protect aid workers and prevent the outbreak of further warfare, the Burundi military and head of state rejected such plans. On this Albright has been clear; a military coup will lead to an international policy of isolation of Burundi and a wholesale stoppage of all but the most meager aid.

Most observers agree that during a time when the majority of the foreign policy ministers in the major countries were preoccupied with developments in the Baltics and the Middle East, Madeleine Albright was light-years ahead of everyone in foreseeing the coming troubles in Africa. One senior White House official remarked, "With Madeleine's background, it came as no surprise to anybody that she was the first one to focus in on Africa." Recently she told friend Jesse Helms, "I visited a beautiful part of Rwanda, where they filmed *Gorillas in the Mist*. Not far from there is an old stone church. By its side, American and other volunteers work with little brushes to clean and reassemble the skeletons of people slaughtered there in 1994. Among the hundreds of skeletons there, I happened to notice one in particular that was only two feet long, about the size of my little grandson." Taking a moment, the ambassador paused to collect her emotions. "You know, they say in the foreign policy business, we aren't supposed to let ourselves be influenced by emotion, but how can we forget that murdered children are not emotions, but that they are human beings whose potential contributions are forever lost."

In response to the ongoing instability in Africa, Albright has spearheaded the administration's plan for an African Crisis Response Force. For now, as reported by many news sources, Rwanda today is comparatively stable, with a new government making steady progress toward restoring order and infrastructure, as its war-ravaged economy has experienced a 40 percent expansion during the last year.

Other global imperatives commanding Albright's attention during her time at the United Nations included the Middle East, Northern Ireland, the North Korean nuclear threat, and NATO expansion.

Although then-Secretary of State Warren Christopher made it clear during the early days of the Clinton administration that the Middle East was his exclusive purview, he was nevertheless faced with the indisputable reality that whatever strategy the White House embraced, support of the UN Security Council was a vital component of any successful strategy. During the first two years of the Clinton administration, Secretary Christopher must have logged countless air miles shuttling between Tel Aviv, Cairo, Riyadh, Damascus, and Washington, as he sought to build a comprehensive peace in the region. And there were some successes. If one image could symbolize the Clinton administration's efforts and commitment in this troubled corner of the world, it would be the famous handshake of peace between Yasir Arafat and Yitzhak Rabin. There, on September 13, 1993, the two leaders celebrated an agreement to remove Israeli troops from Arab towns and cities in the occupied West Bank and to grant self-rule by the middle of 1996. And despite the tragic assassination of Prime Minister Rabin, further negotiations have moved toward granting

Palestinians autonomy in return for security guarantees. Other diplomatic successes include the Israeli-Palestinian Treaty; the Israeli-Jordanian Peace Accord; the Summit of Peacemakers in Egypt with twenty-nine world and regional leaders gathered to support the Middle East peace process and to counter terrorism; securing a written agreement between Israel and Syria to end Hezbollah attacks on Israel and provide security to civilians on both sides of the Lebanon-Israel border.

And while Secretary Christopher was playing the very public role of shuttle diplomat, Ambassador Albright for her part assumed a vital, behind-the-scenes role, quietly building coalitions in support of the peace process with the various nations to which peace in the Middle East is of vital interest. Ironically, she had the greatest level of success in dealing with the delegates and senior officials from the many Islamic nations in the region, which found her open-mindedness refreshing for an American. While steadfastly committed to Israel's security, Albright let it be known that, in her view, the politics of the Middle East was a multifaceted puzzle and far more complex than simply taking steps to protect Israeli borders. Well aware that with the exception of the Israelis, Saudi Arabia was America's strongest ally in the region, she willingly listened for hours to various members of the Saudi delegation express Riyadh's concerns on a host of issues, not just Israel. "It might surprise you to know," she would tell a colleague at the State Department, "that the House of Saud holds no affection whatsoever for Saddam Hussein. And that they are far less concerned with an Israeli attack than the Iraqis."

As for the Iraqi dictator, there seems to be nothing Albright likes better than to deliver regular reality checks to Saddam. Take the time in 1995, when Saddam mobilized troops near the Kuwaiti border. That same day, on the floor of the General Assembly the Iraqi ambassador attempted to justify his country's actions by describing the troop maneuvers as defensive, based on intelligence reports of an expected American invasion. Ambassador Albright, barely able to keep a straight face, retorted that the envoy's speech was "the most ridiculous speech she had ever heard," and characterized Saddam's foreign policy since his Gulf War defeat as "four years of lies."

The next day, the official Iraqi newspaper called her a "snake," and vowed that Iraq would never withdraw its troops. About an hour later, President Clinton dispatched a full reserve of US planes, warships—including the battleship *New Jersey*—and ground troops to the region.

After American F-14s downed two of their aircraft and a military installation was destroyed by US artillery fire, Iraqi generals ordered an immediate retreat. By nightfall, every Iraqi troop had withdrawn from the region.

At a recent speech at Georgetown University, Albright also sent a signal to those who would have the United States withdraw economic sanctions against Iraq. The message was clear. Don't even think about it. "As long as Saddam is in power, the position of the United States will remain unchanged. It is the right policy. But if a new government were to come to power in Baghdad, the US would stand ready to enter rapidly into a dialogue with the successor regime." She went on to say that "it is essential, that international resolve not weaken, that Iraq's behavior and intentions must change before our policies can change."

When asked to clarify US policy toward Saudi Arabia, in light of the hard-line stance the US has taken versus Iran and Iraq, Albright explains, "Saudi Arabia is very important to the United States. There's no question about it. They are important to us for our national security interests and we work with them. It is important to us for stability in the Middle East and also, obviously, because of oil. So we do need Saudi Arabia. But our policy on Iran and Iraq is one that we will pursue because we are very concerned about their support of terrorism and what they do in terms of destabilizing the region."

And this is not to say that Albright's relationship with the Arab bloc has been one ongoing love fest. After one particularly long session of listening to the chargé d'affaires from a small, oil-rich kingdom vent, an aide asked Albright, "Ambassador, don't you ever just run out of patience with some of these delegates?"

"Not really, dear," she responded. "Don't forget, I raised three children."

And, in June of 1996, when U.S. Attorney General Janet Reno publicly condemned Saudi officials for failing to cooperate in the investigation of the terrorist bombing of a US military barracks in Riyadh that killed nineteen American soldiers and injured hundreds, Albright took the Saudi ambassador to task, telling him in no uncertain terms that the United States "expects the full assistance of the Saudi government on this matter." When the envoy protested, asking why her country's attorney general was meddling in foreign policy, Albright cut him off. "Make no mistake about it, Mr. Ambassador, the United States government is completely unified on this matter. Janet Reno and Louis Freeh," she said referring to the attorney general and FBI director, respectively, "are in charge of the investigation and we expect your full cooperation in completing the investigation. Period."

In general, Albright sees more potential to achieve peace and promote democracy in the Middle East than ever before. This in spite of the recent rift between Israeli Prime Minister Netanyahu and Palestinian leader Arafat. But she is also aware of the challenge ahead. "Today, there remain two competing visions in the Middle East. One is focused on the grievances and tragedies of the past; the other on the possibilities of the future. We've made great strides through the Hebron agreement, and the importance of that is that Prime Minister Netanyahu and the Palestinian Authority signed an agreement . . . that is the first time that has ever happened. An agreement on Hebron would serve as a catalyst, strengthening the supporters of peace."

Of all the international crises faced by the Clinton administration none portended more serious consequences than the sudden, inexplicable decision by the Republic of North Korea to withdraw from the international Nuclear Non-Proliferation Treaty and deny inspectors from the International Atomic Energy Administration the right to inspect their plutonium processing facilities. What's more, while inspections of North Korean facilities were always problematic—they had continually resisted inspections, calling such scrutiny "inappropriate"—the IAEA became aware of new evidence that the North Korean government was pursuing the development of its own weapons program by acquiring its own technology and fissionable material to construct its own bombs. The growing menace of North Korea as a nuclear power in such a volatile region simply could not be overstated. As *Time* magazine put it, "North Korea is the 1990s equivalent of the Cuban missile crisis."

In 1993, when North Korea made the unexpected announcement, the Clinton administration threatened the Pyongyang regime with worldwide diplomatic and economic isolation, reminding them of America's role should North Korea ever attack South Korea. At the United Nations, Ambassador Albright laid out in stark terms the commitment of the US to defend South Korea if war broke out, and pledged that the combined forces of the two nations "would decisively and rapidly defeat any attack from the North. The US could not afford to sit back idly and do nothing," she claimed, as North Korea proceeded with its nuclear program.

At this point it was estimated that North Korea would have enough plutonium to produce five or six nuclear bombs by the end of 1994. In addition to South Korea, there was a potential threat to Japan and Taiwan if North Korea developed delivery systems.

The Clinton administration believed that if efforts to halt North Korea's nuclear buildup failed, other renegade states intent on building such weapons could be encouraged to proceed with their programs. For months both Secretary of State Warren Christopher and Ambassador Albright pursued diplomatic avenues to resolve the crisis. Then in June of 1994, with little hope in sight, the US announced a two-prong proposal for sanctions designed, in Albright's words, to "deliver a political message to North Korea that it needs to make an adjustment in its behavior. The more they break the rules, the tougher the sanctions." And while the proposal, which included a mandatory arms embargo and UN controls on cargo flights, was being showcased back in Washington, Albright for her part began an intensive round of negotiations with the fourteen other Security Council nations in the hope of heading off any potential veto threat. Of particular concern was the People's Republic of China, which besides being an ally of the North Koreans, also carried veto authority as a permanent member of the Security Council. In order to coax them on board, the measure was carefully crafted to include a grace period of several weeks to allow North Korea to modify its position and thereby avoid sanctions.

On June 20, 1994, North Korea responded that it would "never allow inspections" of two suspected nuclear waste sites and warned that sanctions would lead to war. In response, Albright gave the North Koreans two choices: continue their nuclear weapons program and face the consequences, possibly including war, or drop it and accept economic aid and normal relations with the US and its allies.

China, in a bit of maneuvering, upped the ante somewhat, still taking the public position of being opposed to sanctions. Together the President, Christopher, and

Albright met, each concluding that the Chinese were bluffing. With this mind-set the Clinton administration went forward with plans to put the issue of sanctions before the UN Security Council for a vote, as a wary South Korea stepped up civil-preparedness measures.

Three days later, North Korea relented, agreeing to freeze its nuclear program. High-level talks would resume in Geneva between the two countries, aimed at a comprehensive settlement of the North Korean nuclear issues in return for closer diplomatic and economic ties between the US and North Korea.

As a result of the confrontation, North Korea agreed to fully abide by the Nuclear Non-Proliferation Treaty, including allowing inspectors access to any of its facilities. But while the outcome of the tense yearlong series of negotiations was successful, many foreign policy observers fail to truly understand that an extraordinary feat of diplomacy had taken place. One congressman said of the crisis, "The real threat, if the North Koreans are allowed to get more nuclear-weapons material, would be their selling it, not using it. Their economy is virtually nonexistent. They'll do anything for money, which is why they're the largest exporter of Scud missiles." The true brilliance of the deal, however, was not in what the US achieved, but what it left in place. From the beginning, Madeleine Albright, echoing Ronald Reagan's admonition to "trust but verify," favored the position that in order to resolve the crisis, any agreement must focus on the North Koreans' future capability. While it would be desirable to get an assessment of the outlaw republic's immediate nuclear resources, any such inquiry would probably have chased Pyongyang away from the negotiating table. By allowing the North Koreans to retain some capability—that is, some of its already processed plutonium—in exchange for the discontinuation of the reprocessing program, the US achieved its overall objective. Senator Bob Kerrey of Nebraska, one of the top defense minds in the Senate, applauds Albright's deft negotiating skills. "There is no way we would have ever achieved a solution to the North Korean nuclear crisis without Ambassador Albright in there negotiating for the US. From the start her instincts were dead on."

Regarding Northern Ireland, the Clinton administration played a critical role in advancing the peace process in Belfast by acknowledging that Sinn Fein, as the political representative of the Irish Republican Army, had a rightful place at the bargaining table to determine the future of Ulster. The President even went so far as to invite Sinn Fein leader Gerry Adams to the White House on St. Patrick's Day in 1995. With the US State Department granting Adams a visa to enter the country for the visit, it thereby allowed him to raise support and money in the US legally for his cause for the first time. Suffice it to say, given that passions tend to run high when it comes to the centuries-old conflict, this made for some tense moments between Ambassador Albright and the British delegation to the UN. Even more complicated was the fact that almost to a vote, the United States and Britain—both permanent members of the Security Council—are universally aligned on every matter and Albright considered many in the contingent among her close friends. She wished she could retract her oft-cited remark critical of the British style, "tea and crumpets diplomacy."

Nevertheless, these efforts led directly to the Irish Republican Army announcing a unilateral cease-fire in late 1995. Soon thereafter, President Clinton visited Northern Ireland, where he received a hero's welcome, sending the crowd of well-wishers into a near frenzy when he promised US support if the Irish renounced violence and participated in the peace process. President Clinton was represented by former Senator George Mitchell—who lost out in the Foggy Bottom sweepstakes—as his personal representative in the negotiations that resulted in a truce between the British government, the Ulster Defense Association, and the IRA. That cease-fire was broken in April 1996 when the IRA, frustrated at the slow progress in the peace talks, renewed bombings in London. As for Ambassador Albright, this left her in a similar situation to that of the Middle East talks. While another envoy, in this case Senator Mitchell, working alongside the American ambassador to Ireland Patricia Kennedy, was responsible for the public discussions in the disarmament talks, she conducted the behind-the-scenes negotiations to address the concerns of both the British and Irish governments, as well as a new silent partner with a vested interest in the outcome of the talks, the Vatican. Speaking regularly with the Pope in his native Polish, Albright regarded him as a head of state and readily accepted the Pontiff's input on how to resolve the conflict, including a proposed commitment of humanitarian aid by the Catholic Church if necessary.

Negotiations to resolve the long-standing sectarian conflict resumed in September 1996. To date no new cease-fire agreement is in sight.

A third area of major activity during Albright's tenure as UN ambassador was that of NATO expansion. The North American Treaty Organization was established to present a united front in western Europe to protect that part of the continent against any potential Soviet advance. With the demise of the Soviet Union, the question has been posed whether or not there is any real need for the continued existence of the North American Treaty Organization. President Clinton has said he not only sees a great need for NATO given the rapidly changing developments in Central and Eastern Europe, but also an important opportunity to solidify the peace that NATO countries have fought so hard over the years to achieve.

Toward this end, the President, in 1994, led the way in creating NATO's Partnership for Peace, an agreement whereby the current members of the NATO alliance have committed to an orderly process of expansion, admitting new members while modernizing and strengthening the organization. A stronger NATO, it was reasoned, meant the US would never have to go it alone. At the NATO summit in Madrid last July, Albright expounded even further. "The purpose of enlargement is to do for Europe's east what NATO did fifty years ago for Europe's west: to integrate new democracies, defeat old hatreds, provide confidence in economic recovery, and deter conflict. Those who say NATO enlargement should wait until a military threat appears miss the main point. NATO is not a Wild West posse that we mobilize only when grave danger is near. It is a permanent alliance, a linchpin of stability, designed to prevent serious threats from ever arising."

Already, results are positive. In Bosnia, soldiers from more than a dozen partner states have joined with US and NATO troops. And in fact, Hungary, the former Soviet satellite, is the major staging ground for the American troops serving in Bosnia.

With the expansion and effective redefinition of NATO, old unnatural alliances were severed and new, logical coalitions and defensive agreements were cemented in place. To Albright, this was an idea whose time had been long overdue. "To those who worry about enlargement dividing Europe, I say that NATO cannot and should not preserve the old Iron Curtain as its eastern frontier. That was an artificial division, imposed upon proud nations, some of which are now ready to contribute to the continent," she says. However, that along with a larger, broader, stronger NATO carries with it a host of new problems for the United States. Under the old alliance, any attack on a NATO member (e.g. Britain) would be viewed by the United States as an attack on its own soil, and it would respond accordingly. Under the new arrangement the same rules apply, but the organization will include as new members Poland, Hungary, and the Czech Republic. As one might expect, the prospect of the United States coming to the rescue of a former eastern bloc nation, makes the former Soviet Union, secure for half a century within its Cold War borders, more than a little nervous.

Most analysts agree that the biggest challenge to fulfillment of NATO expansion by the President's stated target of 1999 is winning over the Russian Republic's President, Boris Yeltsin. Fortunately for the President, when it comes to dealing with Boris Yeltsin, the United States has a secret weapon named Madeleine Albright. As one senior White House official put it, "There's no question about it. Boris Yeltsin genuinely likes the President, but he loves Madeleine."

During her four years at the UN, Albright and Yeltsin had numerous occasions to work and spend large amounts of time together, during his visits to Washington and her trips to Moscow. Sources close to both describe Yeltsin's affection for the ambassador as that of the little sister he never had. Others, who have witnessed Albright's subtle ability to curb the Russian leader's often bawdy public behavior without offending him, view her more like the big sister he's always needed. At any rate, the head of state clearly trusts her, taking Albright at her word when she says to him, of NATO expansion, speaking perfect Russian, that "after World War II we did a great deal for Europe with the Marshall Plan and tried to get countries to work together. We need to do for Central and Eastern Europe what was done for Western Europe after the Second World War; that is, try to provide some sense of stability, try to make sure that ethnic conflicts and border disputes don't overwhelm. NATO expansion is not anti-Russian."

Indeed, Albright, a refugee who grew up watching a country collapse around her, feels great empathy for the challenges facing Yeltsin, recently remarking, "We know that Russia remains in the midst of a wrenching transition, but gains made during the past five years are increasingly irreversible. Despite the threats posed by corruption and crime, open markets and democratic institutions have taken hold. President Yeltsin's challenge in his second term will be to restore the momentum behind the internal reforms and accelerate Russia's integration with the west."

Ironically, during a presidential visit to Europe in 1994, Secretary of State Christopher brushed aside protocol and suggested that Ambassador Albright, not he, escort President Clinton from Air Force One to the arrival ceremonies in Prague. As they walked toward her friend, Czech President Václav Havel, Albright turned to the President and beamed: "It doesn't get any better than this!" In point of fact, she was vastly underestimating her future. Indeed, it would get better, much better in the coming years.

Of the many compelling experiences and accomplishments of Ambassador Madeleine Albright during her time at the United Nations, few were as impressive and surprising as her ability to cultivate and maintain a positive and productive relationship with the Senate Foreign Relations Committee. Beginning with her confirmation hearings and lasting through the 1994 Republican takeover of Congress, the dialogue between Albright's shop and the Committee was characterized by a healthy give-and-take on a multitude of issues as well as positive, frequent communication. And while this certainly is impressive, to anyone who knows Albright, this should not be surprising. Not only was the newly appointed ambassador determined to have a positive relationship with the panel, but she began to build her bridge to the committee two decades earlier.

The year was 1972. The setting was the Muskie for President campaign. It was two weeks before the New Hampshire primary. Money was already growing tight at the campaign and 99 percent of the campaign still lay ahead. And then Madeleine Albright showed up. "Up until that point, outside of a few people who knew her in college, nobody had ever really heard of Madeleine, particularly not as a fund-raiser," said longtime friend and Muskie veteran, Jim Davidson. As many tell the story, one day Albright walks in, this tiny, unassuming young woman, a volunteer no less, and in a matter of weeks, the entire fund-raising operation had been completely turned around. "From the second she showed up, it was clear that Madeleine was a very aggressive and very effective fund-raiser," continues Davidson. "Better than anyone we had seen in a long time."

Although Muskie lost the nomination, the friendship between Albright and the senator endured. So much so that, in 1975, with Muskie facing the toughest reelection challenge of his career, the first person he called was Madeleine Albright. Besides being relentless in her pursuit of major donors, many of whom inhabited the universe of wealth surrounding the Albright family's publishing fortune, she was one of the few people with real knowledge and access to the major donors in the 1972 Muskie presidential campaign. This network, representing a virtual who's who of liberals that contributed heavily to political races, was an indispensable commodity to every major campaign during that election year. A second reason that Albright was an invaluable resource to the campaign was her unique and strong relationship with Senator Muskie and his wife, Jane; a relationship that proved vital in the coming years for Albright as she and the rest of the Muskie team navigated rough waters with the Senator. Finally, the third factor in Albright's indispensability to the reelection campaign was that she had spent years cultivating relationships not just with the money people, but virtually every key activist and elected official in Maine that was close to Ed Muskie.

With Albright on board handling the money, the senator's reelection campaign went into high gear as longtime Muskie Chief of Staff Leon Billings headed the operation. Although this was a relatively new experience for Albright, for Billings and the rest, it was altogether unbelievable. After all, despite his failure to gain the Democratic presidential nomination, Senator Edmund Muskie was still one of the last true giants of politics, especially in Maine. The best the Republicans could do in eighteen years was mount token opposition. But this time around was different. This time the state GOP was running a thoroughbred in the race. A tall, handsome, articulate, moderate young congressman who had been completely untainted by the major issue of the period, Watergate, during two terms in the House. In a truly ironic twist, that young congressman turned out to be none other than William Cohen, who went on to become senator and most recently Secretary of Defense William Cohen, a current colleague of Albright's in the Clinton cabinet. Last spring, Albright and Cohen made their first joint appearance by a Secretary of State and a Secretary of Defense on NBC's *Meet the Press* since the Johnson presidency to discuss a host of issues, but primarily focusing on the Chemical Weapons Treaty. "Talk about coming full circle," Albright would later remark to friends.

As it turned out, the frenzied rush to build a war chest was unnecessary as Cohen, seeing the incumbent's operation expand tenfold in a matter of weeks, declined to run. Instead, the Republicans nominated multimillionaire Robert Monks, who spent millions of his own dollars on his campaign. In the end, it wasn't even close, as Muskie was reelected by a wide margin, spending only about $250,000 to secure the seat.

In 1976, Albright was brought in as an entry-level legislative assistant to the senator, once again under the direction of Billings. Getting the job was a mixed blessing at first. While it was a key step in the reinvention of Madeleine Albright, it was hardly the plum assignment she had hoped for. Moreover, the culture in the senator's office left something to be desired. The senator was well known to have a volcanic temper and a style in dealing with aides that bordered on prosecutorial. Regularly he would warn staff that, "I want to know everything everybody else knows about this—and more." To many, working for Muskie amounted to training with Jesuits, dissecting one's faith and then reassembling it. On the other hand, Muskie was honest, decent, brilliant, and an idealist who could inspire loyalty among his staff and colleagues like few others.

"Madeleine's stint with Muskie really could have gone either way," said one fellow staffer. Billings described it this way: "There were times that some on the staff were so afraid of him that they would literally run away and hide. I would then have to track them down and explain that it didn't work that way, that we couldn't run the office with people hiding from the senator." But for Albright, never one to be intimidated, things seemed to work out. She seemed instantly to become an expert at standing her ground and putting up with Muskie's intimidating manner. "That she could put up with his temper actually served to make Muskie perceive Madeleine as more of a peer than a staffer," said Billings. "In an office that was always scrambling as the senator seemed to live crisis to crisis, Albright never, ever lost her sense of humor. Equally important, she managed to take Muskie with a grain of salt."

Another Muskie veteran echoes the description of Albright's resolve. "Given that Madeleine was the only woman on our foreign policy team, it really took the senator a long time before he was comfortable even muttering a four letter word under his breath when she was around. But when he finally did, she didn't blink. Muskie considered her one of us."

On a policy level the setup was unusual in that most of the advocacy issues—budget, environment, education, and welfare—had large committee staffs and Muskie was said to be more apt to rely on them than his own staff in those areas. But when it came to foreign relations, an area about which he felt passionately and held a direct interest, he looked closer to home. According to Billings, although she was not hired for that purpose, the foreign policy role just fell to Albright because her credentials filled a vacuum. Without her uncanny ability to deal with the senator on a one-to-one basis, it might not have worked out. But it did and in a short period of time Albright went from legislative assistant to legislative director to his chief foreign policy advisor.

And as picture perfect as her evolution as a Capitol Hill operative may have appeared, it was in many respects, one of the most unlikely success stories on record, particularly when you consider that Albright came to the Hill just shy of her fortieth birthday. Her age, along with her gender put Albright in the position of having to break through not one but two glass ceilings simply to begin her career. As any contemporary of that era will attest, while some of the barriers of sex discrimination were, in fact, beginning to soften, most of the opportunities that were available to women in politics were still entry level, the types of positions offering a level of compensation more suited to young people in the early stages of their careers. And Dr. Albright, who had obtained her Ph.D. during this period, was not exactly a conventional fit. Nevertheless, she was determined to defy the odds. Even though she had minimal experience as a fund-raiser, Albright, in the words of Billings, "decided to reinvent herself, taking on the toughest, most uninspiring challenge in the business. The scutwork of politics. For her to even take on that challenge to break into politics simply took incredible gumption." By almost every account, Madeleine Albright did this because, at the time, it may have been her only viable avenue into the world of power politics. And typically, she did it better than anyone else, making people take notice in order to open doors that surely would have remained closed.

Even more incredible was the fact that Albright came to Washington in search of a niche, yet grounded neither her credentials, nor her professional relationships in one specific area or universe. As Billings puts it, "Most people come to Washington from a single sphere and they operate within that sphere once they are here. Lawyers are identified as lawyers, congressional staffers are congressional staffers and so forth." But not Albright. Not only has she always circulated among multiple universes throughout her career, but she has somehow managed to cultivate networks of valuable relationships in each, being viewed by many as the ultimate generalist. In a town in which specialization has traditionally been equated with success, Albright did it her way.

And she certainly did so with Muskie, coming from a Ph.D. program at Columbia, serving as a fund-raiser, finally becoming the foreign policy wonk for the senator. As her former boss points out, "This pattern continued through her career as she went on to the National Security Council Staff, to Georgetown, the Center for National Policy, to the United Nations. At any given time Madeleine's orbit included universes as disparate as foreign policy, academia, fund-raising, and Capitol Hill."

As if this stage of her career wasn't enough of a challenge, Albright's true trial by fire came in 1978 when the Carter administration's National Security Council Advisor, Zbigniew Brzezinski, her international relations professor and mentor while at Columbia, asked her to join him at the NSC as his head of congressional liaison. Under any other set of circumstances, the choice to move over was a no-brainer. More prestige, more responsibility, and not that she needed it, more money. But unfortunately for Albright, Senator Muskie and Brzezinski could not stand the sight of each other. Whether it was a professional rivalry or a personal feud, the animosity between the two men was as palpable as it was public.

Some said the friction had to do with their utter contempt for the other's foreign policy views. Muskie was a true liberal in his worldview, believing in measured responses to the major issues of the day, Afghanistan, the Polish Solidarity movement, and later the Iranian hostage crisis. He was by nature hesitant to commit to the use of force. Brzezinski, on the other hand, was the ultimate hawk, making no secret of his position that any threat to the national interests of the United States needed to be met head-on with a response of equal or greater severity, including the use of lethal force if necessary. In this respect, Albright was clearly aligned with Brzezinski, as she was far more of a hawk than Ed Muskie ever was. Others suggest that the root of the Muskie-Brzezinski rivalry stemmed from the NSC advisor's view, as a Polish-American, that the senator was not, in his opinion, sufficiently "Polish." To Brzezinski, whose family had emigrated from Poland, and who had grown up with his parents recounting vivid memories of living under the totalitarian regime in Warsaw, Muskie's lack of passion in dealing with the Soviet Union was intolerable. But Muskie was born in the United States and raised in Maine in an assimilated household in which Polish was not spoken, only English. It was only during the presidential campaign of 1972 that the senator rediscovered his Polish roots.

For Albright, who understood the refugee experience perhaps better than anybody, this was a horribly tense and difficult situation. And despite the fact that she would joke to others about her dilemma, claiming that she was the only woman in Washington who could go "Pol to Pol," everyone around her was aware how much it hurt for Albright to be caught in the middle of such a contentious battle of egos. Worse, these two larger-than-life figures were both people whom she deeply admired and considered friends. Moreover, the situation became further complicated late in Carter's term when the President tapped Muskie to replace Cyrus Vance as Secretary of State.

Speculation quickly mounted that Albright would jump ship and rejoin her boss at the State Department. And even though she certainly found the option attractive, Albright quickly moved to quell the rumors. As Billings tells it, she was clear on the subject, telling anyone who asked, "This is the choice I made, and as long as I am working for Zbig, I will not take sides." Most who knew her were not surprised. "It was classic Madeleine. Absolutely loyal to a fault," said one colleague close to the situation.

As the Carter term ran out, it is uncertain whether or not Albright continued to second-guess herself about the decision to join the NSC. But one thing is clear. During her time working for Muskie and alongside the Senate Foreign Relations Committee, she built bridges to every single person around her, from the senior staff like Leon Billings to the lowliest intern. "Madeleine was always available, no task was too small. If there was any way she could help out and she had the time, Madeleine would drop what she was doing and pitch in. A lot of people on the staff just looked up to her, particularly the younger ones," said former colleague and ex-congressman Eliot Levitas. Albright's unusually candid relationship with Muskie also went a long way. One staffer said, "Muskie wanted to review everything from the office supply inventory to the latest version of a draft piece of legislation. Sometimes it was impossible to get sign-off on anything because the senator hadn't reviewed it." But when crunch time came Albright was known to go to bat for her colleagues, doing whatever it took to get Muskie to focus on the matter at hand. "I can remember one time that I had been working on a piece of legislation for two months," reminisces Davidson. "I was only twenty-seven years old. Time was running out to get the bill into committee before Congress was to take its spring recess. If I didn't get the senator's signature on it that day, it was going to the bottom of the pile for sure. Try as I might, I couldn't get in to see Muskie, who was preparing for a long-anticipated trip back to his home state and was dealing with a thousand other matters. Finally, it's around six-thirty and he starts to march out, suitcase in hand. Madeleine could see the look on my face and just said, 'Give it to me.' I'll never forget what she did. She ran after the senator, got in front of him as he was standing in front of the Members elevator and in a strident tone, instructed him, 'Don't ask questions. Just sign it.' At first he looked at her like she was crazy. But after a few seconds, realizing she wasn't moving and he couldn't win, he just grabbed the bill and signed it. He trusted her that much."

And while such stories of Albright's days on the Hill have practically risen to the level of urban folklore, a few key elements should not be overlooked. First, it is not so much what Madeleine Albright accomplished during those years as the way she accomplished it. From her first day as a volunteer on the Muskie campaign to the last day of the Carter administration, Albright took great professional and personal risk by injecting herself into unfamiliar terrain and, once there, dedicated herself to the betterment of the larger group, whether it was a campaign, a congressional staff, or the NSC. At each juncture she built friendships that would succeed, occupational boundaries and professional relationships that would endure throughout her career. Simply put, she did a lot of favors for a lot of people and asked nothing in return. As the years passed, many young staffers on the Foreign Relations Committee spent their entire careers in service to the committee. Still others had affiliated with powerful senators who had risen to become senior members of the panel. At any rate, when the time came for Madeleine Albright to face her first confirmation hearing as President Clinton's nominee as ambassador to the United Nations, any worries that the White House may have had concerning Republican opposition were completely unfounded. The fact was that no matter who was serving on the Foreign Relations Committee at any given time, in any given partnership, one simply couldn't serve on the committee staff without having heard of Madeleine Albright. To the senior staff who remembered her twenty years earlier she was a friend and a mentor. To the fresh-faced young staffers she was a legend. Ironically, when it came to her confirmation, it really didn't matter what the senators on the panel thought. As Senator Muskie put it shortly before his death, "When she was nominated, Madeleine came to me for advice about confirmation. I asked around and then called her back. The fact was she didn't need my help. She had the whole committee wired."

5

KILLING
THE MESSENGER

Operation Restore Hope

and the Tragedy at Mogadishu

The scene was horrific. A near-naked body of a dead US Army Ranger, clad only in his green GI issue briefs, being dragged down a crowded street by an angry mob. On each side of the street, screaming onlookers pelted the young soldier's body with rocks and broken bottles as it passed by. Even more hideous, some in the mob, who were burning American flags, attempted to use them as makeshift torches as they tried to set the body on fire. Not since Saigon and Beirut had scenes from a war zone hit so close to home. But it wasn't either of those places and it wasn't supposed to be a war zone. It was a humanitarian mission called Operation Restore Hope, in a place called Somalia.

This soldier was one of eighteen US Army Rangers who died that day, October 3, 1993, to be exact, in Mogadishu during an aborted attempt by American forces to capture Somali warlord General Muhammad Farah Aidid. As the footage filled the airwaves on every major network, the entire country felt revulsion and outrage, especially the President, who was so stunned by the unexpected carnage and the needless waste of life during a peacekeeping mission that he immediately summoned his defense secretary, Les Aspin, to the Oval Office. There, as aides tell it, a near-ballistic President Clinton demanded an explanation. "Les, how could this have happened?" he said. With Aspin's answer the finger-pointing began. To a man, no one would accept responsibility, with virtually everyone pointing his finger elsewhere. Everyone, that is, but Madeleine Albright.

In the wake of the Somalia fiasco, damage control became the order of the day in Washington—including White House spin, Defense Department spin, Foggy Bottom spin, not to mention an international public relations campaign by UN Secretary General Boutros Boutros-Ghali. Suffice it to say, with all the official versions of the incident floating around town, discerning what really happened regarding the US-Somalia initiative has been no easy task. Nevertheless, a synthesis of the varying accounts provides the following time line:

By mid-1992, just before the major party nominating conventions, the situation in Somalia had deteriorated into a full-scale civil war among rival clans and subclans. Absent institutional humanitarian assistance, thousands of Somalis were dying every day from disease and starvation, with hundreds of thousands doomed to a similar fate unless something was done. International relief efforts were so paltry and disorganized that rogue Somali gangs, under orders of the warlords, attacked UN facilities at will, absconding with food, fuel, and medical supplies.

As for the United Nations, the organization's hands were officially tied as warlord Farah Aidid rejected the proposed UN Operation in Somalia, dubbed UNOSOM. Under UN regulations, the operation could not go forward without the unanimous consent of all the parties to the conflict. Tensions continued to mount until just after the November elections, when the Bush State Department weighed in, supporting the dispatch of a major UN military operation to Somalia, which, alongside American troops, would oversee the distribution of humanitarian aid. The Bush administration plan included an American-led coalition that would be replaced after a period of months with a UN force. At the time the United States was prepared to mobilize a total of thirty thousand troops to secure ports, airports, roads, and distribution centers in central and southern Somalia. Why undertake such an ambitious foreign policy initiative so late in a president's term, some may ask? The explanation: according to several senior Bush administration officials, at least part of the motivation for the aggressive posture in Somalia was that President Bush wanted to go out in a blaze of glory as a world statesman. *Newsweek* even reported that many in the Bush White House saw the Somalia initiative as a sort of therapy for the lame duck President, who had been in a funk after losing the election.

Notwithstanding the fact that then-Secretary of State Lawrence Eagleburger made it clear that the US commitment was short term—that there were no guarantees that the incoming Clinton administration would continue the operation—UN Secretary General Boutros Boutros-Ghali was optimistic, saying "such a force could obtain stability very quickly. I know Somalia. I have been there many times." In retrospect, it might have been advisable if Boutros-Ghali had heeded the warning of US ambassador to neighboring Kenya, Smith Hempstone, who characterized the situation as follows: "The Somalis are natural-born guerrillas. They will mine roads. They will lay ambushes. They will launch hit-and-run attacks."

As December approached the UN Security Council considered a number of options, some of a humanitarian nature, others involving an enforcement component. Ultimately, the Council unanimously adopted Resolution 794 on December 9, 1992, embracing Eagleburger's initial proposal for limited US involvement. On December 9, 1992, American troops entered Somalia, and notwithstanding the clear proclamation of limited US involvement, Boutros-Ghali wasted no time in telling all who would listen that he foresaw a much broader role for the United States in the conflict. To the Secretary General, the American mission objective included the disarming of all Somali factions, as well as such functions as defusing the countless land mines throughout the secessionist north and developing a regimen of training for civilian police. Despite this, however, Boutros-Ghali made no attempt to conceal his true feelings toward the United States, saying, "All my experience tells me not to trust the US. You are unpredictable and change your minds too often."

Soon a rift developed between the military cultures at the United Nations and the US Department of Defense. This stemmed from the fact that expanding the scope of the operation inevitably meant delaying the withdrawal of an American military presence in Somalia. In spite of this, however, Boutros-Ghali still viewed UNOSOM II as a traditional UN-style peacekeeping operation, small in scale. Pentagon leaders, on the other hand, scoffed at the idea, knowing that such an operation simply would not be sufficient to get the job done.

The conflict in strategy remained unresolved by the time the Clinton administration assumed control of the White House on January 20, 1993. For weeks little changed as the White House remained generally committed to the objectives established by the Bush administration regarding Somalia, particularly the transitioning of responsibility in the region to the United Nations-sponsored UNOSOM II. Some found this ironic, given that, to the extent Clinton had campaigned on foreign policy, he had embraced a doctrine known as "assertive multilateralism," which, in contrast to the Powell Doctrine, supports a broader usage of military force than simply vindicating vital national interests. One of the chief proponents of assertive multilateralism was Madeleine Albright, who has long held the view that the restoration of democracy and the deposing of dictators fell to the United States as the last remaining superpower.

Within the month, increased fighting among the

warring factions began to make the possibility of an American pullout in the near term all the more unlikely. The situation became further complicated on March 26, 1993, when Boutros-Ghali secured passage of Security Council Resolution 814 that committed the UN to the "maintenance of a secure environment in Somalia." Without ceremony, the White House national security team officially modified its position, having reached an agreement with Boutros-Ghali on an accelerated timetable for American withdrawal and transition to UN control of the operation. With this understanding in mind, Albright spoke for the administration, "With this resolution, we will embark on an unprecedented enterprise aimed at nothing less than the restoration of an entire country as a proud, functioning, and viable member of the community of nations." This statement, while intended to be nothing more than a vote of confidence in the UN initiative, was interpreted as drawing a line in the sand and quite unexpectedly would come back to haunt both the administration and Albright in the coming months.

As the US committed to leaving roughly 9,000 troops behind, the official transition to UNOSOM II was delayed until May 4. While this itself was a setback, the Rubicon was crossed when on June 5 more fighting erupted as Somali rebels, under the command of General Aidid, attacked a Pakistani contingent of UNOSOM II, killing twenty-three soldiers and wounding countless additional troops. For Boutros-Ghali, the conflict had now become personal. Letting his outrage cloud his thinking, the next day the secretary general, together with UN Special Envoy Admiral

Jonathan Howe pushed for a resolution authorizing the immediate arrest of Aidid. Effectively, in an attempt to show the world that the United Nations could not be pushed around by some small-time warlord, the two men took the decidedly undiplomatic step of putting a bounty on Aidid's head. This was a particularly absurd undertaking, given that Aidid was the man largely responsible for ousting Somali dictator Mohammed Siyad Barre from power and held almost legendary status in many parts of the war-ravaged land. Albright herself was growing increasingly uneasy with Boutros-Ghali's priorities. A number of UN officials echoed her concern, describing Boutros-Ghali's stance on the capture of Aidid as bordering on an obsession. It was at this point, by choosing to oppose Aidid militarily, that the United Nations forfeited the right to serve as an honest broker of peace between the warring factions. By Boutros-Ghali's severe and, some say, irrational actions, UNOSOM II and the remaining contingent of American forces were effectively backed into a corner, relegated to performing their nation-building function under combat conditions for the next several months.

For most of the summer, military operations continued, with mixed reports coming out of Mogadishu. According to the Defense Department, Aidid's forces had been severely damaged, his hold on power badly weakened. On the other hand, the Red Cross civilian fatality numbers were as high as anything ever seen on the continent. Back home, furious debate ensued with the administration taking hits from the leaders of both parties, all of whom demanded an immediate withdrawal from the region. Still the

President resisted, determined to stay the course. In late August, Defense Secretary Aspin delivered a major address in which he claimed, "We went there to save a people, and we succeeded. We are staying there now to help those same people rebuild their nation." This declaration, along with Ambassador Albright's earlier statement of support were immediately seized upon by critics of administration foreign policy and they were both vilified in the press.

Militarily, the last major turning point came on September 14, when the US Commander on the Ground in Somalia, Major General Thomas Montgomery, made an official request for heavy armor, including tanks and Bradley fighting vehicles, to support US ground troops who were coming under heavy fire. The request was relayed to Aspin by Joint Chiefs Chairman Colin Powell, who according to *Newsweek* contributing editor, Colonel David Hackworth, "failed to support the request strongly enough to keep Aspin from spiking it." On the diplomatic front, things got even hotter for Albright when the administration lent its backing to Security Council Resolution 865 on September 22, continuing "nation-building" operations until 1995. Three days later, acting under orders from one of the warlords, Somali ground forces shot down a US Black Hawk helicopter, killing three American servicemen. With the pressure mounting for the administration to clarify its policy regarding the UN peacekeeping operation, President Clinton himself addressed the UN General Assembly, spelling out just how far the US was willing to go in support of UNOSOM II. And while the President's speech allayed the fears of many, its benefit was short-lived.

At 3:30 P.M. on October 3, amid intelligence reports tracing the whereabouts of warlord Farah Aidid to the Olympic Hotel in downtown Mogadishu, a team of one hundred US Army Rangers, supported by twelve Black Hawk helicopters, launched a raid in an attempt to capture the elusive general. After capturing nineteen prisoners, American forces were ambushed by Somali militiamen. By days end, three helicopters were downed and eighteen Americans were dead. Aidid escaped unharmed.

It took no time for official Washington to circle the wagons and run for cover in the wake of the tragedy. Les Aspin blamed both the UN and the on-site UNOSOM II commanders for the failure of the mission. Joint Chiefs Chairman General Colin Powell blamed Les Aspin. Boutros-Ghali blamed both of them. Secretary of State Warren Christopher blamed no one, but rather attempted with little success to explain the unfortunate course of events to both the Congress and various news outlets. President Clinton, as Commander in Chief, made no attempt to duck the issue, taking full responsibility for the aborted raid. Ironically, while the President's stoicism was admirable, it may have been misplaced as most observers agree that if there ever was a situation in which a president could pass the buck and get away with it, Somalia was the case. There was no getting around the fact that in this case the President's foreign policy advisors, particularly Les Aspin, had failed him badly, resulting in disastrous consequences.

Meanwhile, back in New York, UN Ambassador Madeleine Albright was back at work, saying virtually nothing on the subject of Somalia. As one of the chief foreign policy spokespersons for the administration, she had gone on record a number of times in support of the US efforts, including authoring an August 10 *New York Times* editorial on the subject, emphasizing the importance of the mission in Somalia, explaining that the humanitarian goals of the operation were unattainable without a secure environment. To the public and the media, Albright played a key role in the failed policy and was so treated in the media onslaught following the Mogadishu raid. *The Washington Post, The New York Times, The Wall Street Journal, Time, Newsweek, US News and World Report* as well as the electronic media all ran stories highlighting her role, in most cases with a decidedly negative slant. "Bad press was one thing, but the treatment of Albright was tantamount to a public hanging," said one State Department official.

What went unreported in the media and unacknowledged by the Clinton administration, was that Albright's role in the decisions pertaining to Somalia had been completely distorted. Rather than being the key player as represented to the public at large, she was proactively excluded from the policy-making process. And, given her high profile position at the United Nations, Albright, whether intentionally or not, was set up as a convenient target for critics of the Clinton administration's Somalia policy. This, despite the fact that, in the words of former Secretary of State Warren Christopher, "Madeleine had absolutely nothing to do with Somalia."

How this could have happened is itself intriguing. It had always been the President's intention that Albright be part of his inner foreign policy circle—as demonstrated by the fact that he elevated her post to cabinet level and named her to the National Security Council. However, a combination of factors led to her virtual exclusion from the first major foreign policy test of the Clinton White House. One element was physical proximity. Despite her constant shuttling between New York and Washington, much of her time in the early months of 1993 was spent attending to the business of the General Assembly and the UN Security Council. But the second and major factor was that the die was cast on the Clinton administration's policy regarding Somalia within days of his election. According to a senior White House official, the decision on Somalia was made back in the days of the transition and not by his foreign policy advisors, but by campaign spinmeisters. "It was one of the most cynical things I've ever seen," said a source close to the '92 transition team. "Instead of consulting with Christopher or Aspin or Albright, the President was being told that their position on Somalia was a no-brainer. Embrace the Bush administration's position. If it works claim credit for it. If it fails we can always blame Bush."

Once they took over, American policy on Somalia became the exclusive purview of Aspin and NSC director Tony Lake. Christopher, recognizing the military component of the mission, deferred to the Defense Department and instead concentrated on pursuing a diplomatic solution with Boutros Boutros-Ghali. The trouble was that, contrary to his public persona, Boutros-Ghali had virtually abandoned hope of a diplomatic solution. Instead, he felt that the importance of a military victory over Aidid far outweighed the benefits of any political solution. Thus, with the Secretary General having sold the White House a bill of goods and the State Department effectively spinning its wheels, the only relevant sphere of policy making was out of Les Aspin's shop. And it was clear that Aspin, along with Powell and General Joseph Hoar, commander of the US Central Command in Somalia (CENTCOM), saw the military taking the lead on the operation. Nevertheless, collectively, the three were hesitant when it came to committing increased firepower to the region, something that would signal an unacceptable military escalation in the conflict.

On the rare occasions that Somalia policy was addressed in the weekly Principals meetings, Albright repeatedly warned that the status of the operation was being undermined by "mission creep"—a symptom in military parlance describing the way an operation can quickly evolve to outgrow and run at cross purposes to its mission objective. Inevitably, the ambassador's opinion would be rejected out of hand, as the White House maintained that Somalia was primarily a Defense matter. What developed was a pattern in which Albright would be asked to exit such meetings and serve as the administration's messenger, selling a policy that she felt was ill-conceived and tactically unsound. And while Albright agreed generally with the goals of the mission, she simply felt that the overall strategy would not work. Nevertheless, always a team player, Albright accepted her role and made every effort to cast the administration's Somalia policy in the best possible light.

Ironically, former Bush administration official John Boltson, in a scathing attack on the Clinton administration's Somalia policy, points to Albright's March 26 speech in support of UN Resolution 814 as irrefutable evidence that it was not mission creep at all, but a deliberate effort by the administration to expand the scope of the operation.

During the aftermath of the tragedy, all the key players took decisive action to mend their relationships with Congress, the media, and minimize the damage to their reputations. But Madeleine Albright could do none of that. To deny her involvement would undermine her credibility among her peers at the UN. To blame Boutros-Ghali would do the same. To blame Aspin or Powell publicly would have the smell of sour grapes and would certainly serve to create a divisive climate in an already divided administration. Sadly, Madeleine Albright, who understood that the two-track policy that Boutros-Ghali had convinced Aspin to follow—to ask Aidid to take the lead in the formulation of a political solution while at the same time hunting him down like a criminal—was a practical impossibility. Painted into a corner, it was Albright who had no choice but to take the hits in the media and the barbs from her colleagues in the General Assembly, effectively playing lightning rod for a badly wounded White House.

Whether or not Albright was ordered to play this role or did so voluntarily is uncertain, although several top administration officials and close friends such as Senator Patrick Leahy insist that they have seen her play this role on other occasions for the good of the team. But whatever led up to Ambassador Albright serving as the administration's target on Somalia, it was a pivotal event in her growth within the Clinton White House. Whether by design or not, Somalia was the first and last time Madeleine would ever allow herself to be out of the loop.

On October 3, 1993, eighteen American servicemen died as a result of a grossly incompetent US strategy regarding Somalia. At the time there were those in the White House who would have preferred that UN Ambassador Madeleine Albright remain a bystander in the formulation and execution of American foreign policy. But on that day, the landscape of American foreign relations changed permanently. To both the President and Secretary of State Warren Christopher, it was no secret who bore the real responsibility for the unraveling of Operation Restore Hope. They were also well aware of who stood up to the media barrage and took the heat and who did not.

From that day forward and for the remainder of her term at the United Nations and through her appointment as Secretary of State, not a single matter or decision regarding the United States internationally has been made without first being run across Albright's desk for feedback or sign-off. By no means has Albright won every battle, but unlike Somalia, in which she was intentionally excluded from the process, Albright now has the President's ear, and more important, his trust.

6

VICTORY IN BOSNIA

The Public Feud with

General Colin Powell and the

Call for a War Crimes Tribunal

The pilot's approach to the narrow landing strip at Tuzla airport was rocky. For more than thirty minutes, the military-style 737 had circled the pre–World War II facility awaiting clearance to land. The fact that the plane had flown into a thunderstorm, with its passengers seeing shrapnel fire shooting up at the plane from ground-based vantage points in the Bosnian countryside didn't make matters easier. The airport, strategically located between two mountains near the rugged Dalmatian coast in Croatia, was an easy target for Serb mortar fire. Well aware that Tuzla airport lacked a modern air traffic radar system, pilots were forced to rely on their own visual analysis or instruments to land their planes. As if this wasn't enough, the airport runway was not only outdated in its construction but dangerously short, roughly two-thirds as long as a standard military airstrip. Translation: there was no way primitive Tuzla airport could accommodate modern military or commercial aircraft, which are bigger and heavier and fly at much greater speeds than vintage WW II dual prop planes. With natural sniper roosts on either side of the main runway, the option of a long, gradual descent to slow the planes' approach, was not viable. Neither was a conventional rectangular flight pattern. In short, flying into Tuzla had grown so dangerous that American pilots had devised a unique and highly risky technique to land their planes, known in aviation parlance as a "rapid descent landing." The unusual maneuver operated as follows: unlike a normal approach, which would begin about a mile out, this method entailed taking the plane in close and ascending to two or three times the normal landing-approach altitude, safely out of mortar range. Then, at the precise moment over the landing area, the plane would begin rapid descent, virtually nosediving in a vertical drop toward the runway at about an eighty-degree angle. At about 1,000 feet the pilot must pull up, level off, and steer the aircraft down the runway, thereby substantially diminishing the plane's speed and reducing the amount of runway needed for landing.

For UN Ambassador Madeleine Albright, who had flown into hundreds of trouble spots and war zones throughout the world, this was even a little more than she could take. Like others in the Clinton administration's foreign policy team, she had been gravely concerned over the rapidly deteriorating situation in the Balkans. For more than a year, she and Secretary of State Warren Christopher had formulated option after option in attempting to bring the warring factions to the negotiating table. But to no avail. For the Republicans, the answer was simple, or in Albright's view, simplistic—lift the arms embargo so that the Bosnian Muslims could defend themselves. But Albright and the rest of the Clinton administration remained convinced that such a move would further inflame the situation, almost certainly escalating the genocide already underway. Months passed with no solution in sight. Pundits continually described the administration's foreign policy as lacking foundation, a study in vacillation, or politically adrift. Every poll showed the President's approval rating dropping precipitously, especially in the area of foreign policy. Then in early 1994 something happened. Something that made it imperative that Madeleine Albright go to Bosnia personally to take stock of the situation. It wasn't a breakthrough solution to the problem or a major concession on the part of the Serbs. Rather, it was *NBC Nightly News.*

Albright was in the middle of a conference call at her office in the UN Building when the footage came over the television. The savagery of the image was unthinkable. Not since the height of Vietnam had footage of such wartime atrocities been broadcast into the American living room. As for the ambassador, who had had the benefit of intermittent intelligence briefings on rumors of Serb atrocities, nothing could have prepared her for what she was about to see. That evening, as NBC correspondent, David Bloom, attempted to put words to the horrific sight, Albright interrupted her phone call, saying, "Forgive me. Something has come up. Is there any way I can call you back?" As she hung up, the ambassador was stunned as she watched the television network depict in gory detail the latest episode of Serbian ethnic cleansing, rebutting with irrefutable evidence the proclamation, "Never Again!"

First on television and only days later in person, Albright's words describe the slaughter. Referring to the trip, she said, "Last year, I visited a farm in what was once a pretty town in Croatia called Vukovar. There, beneath a pile of rusted refrigerators and scraps of farm equipment, is a shallow grave containing the bodies of two to three hundred human beings. Most were adults. But many were teenagers. Some . . . some, it is so sad, were just children, even babies. Shot, stabbed, limbs missing, some had been horribly burned, even decapitated. These dead, like the victims of Srebrenica, Banja Luka, Sarajevo, Mostar, and so many other locations in that torn land, were not the victims of 'the heat of battle' violence. They were not collateral damage. They were intentionally targeted and massacred not because of what they had done but for who they were."

So without a solution in hand and in the face of constant danger, Albright knew she had to go to Bosnia, and go soon. And while she had plenty to fear about flying into Tuzla—Secretary of Commerce Ron Brown, a good friend of Albright's, would die in a fiery plane crash along with thirty-four others on approach to the airport a year later—most of what really posed a threat to Albright was on the ground. As it happened UN Ambassador Madeleine Albright was more than just your average American envoy. She was the daughter of a Czech diplomat who had spent her childhood in Belgrade. But more than this, she had been outspoken in her support of the establishment of a Bosnian War Crimes Tribunal to investigate the unprecedented inhumanity perpetrated at the behest of Serbian strongman Radovan Karadzic. Suffice it to say, that in the locales in the Bosnian conflict, the Serbs, the Bosnian Muslims, and the Croatians were well aware of who Madeleine Albright was and what to expect from her.

No sooner had her convoy left the Tuzla airfield under a military escort than it began. En route to Vukovar, dozens of native Serbs could be seen lined along the narrow asphalt road. Like so many places in Bosnia, Vukovar had only one way in, one way out. As they approached the city, Albright couldn't help but notice the intensity among the bystanders as they spied her motorcade. Every few minutes, sudden, muffled explosions—presumably automatic weapon fire—could be heard in the distance, probably gunfire. And, on a few occasions the lead vehicle of the convoy, a white HUM-V bearing the UN logo, would slow down as it passed a gathering of ethnic Serbs, with the soldier perched atop the vehicle readying his weapon, training it on the crowd just in case.

By the time Albright reached the Croatian city, word of her arrival had swept the countryside. This was not a good thing. As she exited her vehicle, the ambassador suddenly found herself and her entourage the target of yet another angry Serbian mob, with protesters pelting her motorcade with rocks and bottles and screaming obscenities at her. "This is Serbia!" they chanted. Suddenly, when a young aide only a few feet in front of her was hit in the face with a brick, filling his face with blood, Albright had no choice but to advise her staff to retreat, telling them to remain cool, not to show fear, to walk back to the bus in a dignified manner.

As they made their way back, a woman leaped from the crowd, screaming at Albright, "Kucko! Kucko!" The ambassador, who is fluent in five languages including Czech and Russian and knows enough Serbian to get by, knew she was the target of the insult. Translation: "Bitch! Bitch!" When an aide asked her what they were saying, Albright, more concerned with the well-being of her aides, said only, "It's not really important. I think it's time to go. . . ." As the motorcade drove off in a hail of stones, she was the only member of the group to understand the words of the Serbian demonstrators.

After navigating the rugged terrain for several miles, Albright's convoy rendezvoused with Chairman of the Joint Chiefs of Staff General John Shalikashvili, who had been asked by the President to meet Albright on the fact-finding mission. The timing of the trip coincided with the opening of the new American embassy in Sarajevo and it had been decided by the White House that a joint appearance by the pair to christen the new mission would send the right signal to the Bosnians—that the US was unequivocally committed to a resolution of the conflict. As it turned out, the meeting of the two took on a symbolic nature of added dimension, given that Albright was the only US cabinet-level official, and General Shalikashvili was the highest ranking American officer to travel to the war-ravaged country since civil war broke out in 1992.

After departing the rendezvous point together, Shalikashvili, the former allied commander in Europe, wasted little time giving Albright a personal, guided tour of the war zone, including the mass graves on the outskirts of Vukovar. It was at that moment, after seeing what the Serbs were capable of, that Albright's view of the Bosnian civil war underwent a permanent transformation. No longer was she fixated on righting historical wrongs or redrawing political boundaries to appease warring factions. In plain and simple terms, Madeleine Albright saw the mission of the US in Bosnia with absolute clarity, as did Shalikashvili: Stop the genocide. Stop it now!

To truly understand Madeleine Albright's contribution to achieving peace in the Bosnian civil war, it is critical to bear in mind that long before she was named ambassador to the United Nations, the former Yugoslavia had disintegrated into ethnic battle zones over which three warring factions lay claim: Serbs, Croatians, and Bosnian Muslims. Sarajevo, once a host city to the Winter Olympics, had become a virtual no-man's-land. When Albright and Joint Chiefs Chairman Shalikashvili actually conducted the inauguration ceremony of the new US embassy, the sound of automatic weapon fire from the Bosnian Serbs almost drowned out the ambassador's words, echoing John F. Kennedy's speech in Berlin in 1961, when she said, "*Ja sam*

Sarajevka" ("I am a Sarajevan"). Evidence of indescribable acts of brutality by Serb forces appeared everywhere. Information obtained by the UN Security Council substantiated the testimony provided by refugees that almost 8,000 men and boys from Srebrenica had, in fact, been summarily executed as part of an ethnic cleansing order of Bosnian Serb military commander Ratko Mladic.

Despite the tragic and nonstop loss of life, the debate over the specific responsibility of the US to end the conflict had raged on for years. And while many in the administration had hesitated in backing a specific plan, Madeleine Albright's position was clear. Her main historical reference point had long been Munich in 1938 when the Western allies abandoned Czechoslovakia to Adolf Hitler. "Albright has known firsthand what tyranny and totalitarianism can do to ordinary people," said Czech ambassador to Washington Michael Zantovsky. "The lesson of Munich is that you do not appease aggressors, you stick by your friends, and you take a stand for values and what you really believe in."

Thus by 1994, the critical question for Albright, along with Secretary of State Christopher and General Shalikashvili, was no longer whether or not to use military force in Bosnia, but rather a question of when and how. During this visit Albright and Shalikashvili met directly with British army Lt. General Michael Rose, the commander of the UN operation in Bosnia. At the meeting, Shalikashvili emphasized that any US military participation in Bosnia would have to be under NATO command and that UN command of the operation would be entirely unacceptable.

Participants in the meetings attest that while General Rose was at first amenable to US demands, French representatives expressed reservations about relinquishing control of the operation to NATO, which would have the probable result of a new peacekeeping force falling under the authority of a British or American commander. Albright, for her part, made it clear that neither the President nor the nation could accept another Mogadishu. General Shalikashvili concurred, assuring her that such an occurrence simply would not happen on his watch. Together, demonstrating a unique working relationship between warrior and diplomat, the two communicated the US position in blunt terms to the French. "Do not waste any time worrying about who will be in command of American forces should they be committed to the Bosnian theater. Make no mistake about it. American soldiers will serve under an American commander. Period."

Finally, before returning to Washington, Albright and Shalikashvili met with the military leaders of the Muslim and Croatian factions. There, they listened to hours of vitriolic bromides condemning the Serbs. Nevertheless, leaders of both factions expressed their desire to achieve a cease-fire. "They talked peace," said Albright. "But what came through was that they wanted vengeance." Both came away from the meetings with the same conclusion— any lingering doubt that the Republican proposal to arm the Muslims would lead to a bloodbath was erased. The only way to stabilize the situation was to deploy US troops.

So upon their return, and over the persistent cry of congressional Republicans, the Clinton administration made the decision to support the multinational United Nations peacekeeping force, and began the hard work of building the consensus at home for the inevitable troop deployment to Bosnia.

While the UN made some progress—the sustained artillery shelling of Sarajevo's civilian population was temporarily halted, and finally, in the face of overwhelming evidence, a War Crimes Tribunal was established—the killing went on. It was about this time that one UN delegate went before the cameras during an open session of the Security Council and, citing comments by two UN military commanders in Bosnia, attacked the US for encouraging the Muslims, thereby prolonging the war in the Balkans. Albright was quick to respond, suggesting that the anonymous UN commanders "should remember who is paying their salaries." She went on to outline new US efforts to push the peace process forward.

Relying heavily on the counsel of Albright and the negotiating skills of special envoy Richard Holbrooke, President Clinton called for a peace summit to be held in Dayton, Ohio, far removed from war-ravaged Bosnia.

Dayton was the first sit-down negotiation session involving representatives of all three rival factions. And, coming on the heels of US-backed air strikes, achieved momentous breakthroughs. There, the warring parties agreed to accept a single state. The parties, including the Serbs, went further than vague rhetoric. They also accepted the key elements of a sovereign state: a single, clearly defined international border; an internationally recognized central government and United Nations membership; a three-person presidency chosen by direct, free, and internationally supervised elections; a freely elected national assembly; a central bank and a single currency. Moreover, the participants agreed to the formation and compliance with the rulings of a Supreme Court and joint commissions on such matters as railroads, national monuments, and human rights.

While these paper agreements were significant, a number of critical components were successfully implemented on the ground. A devastated Sarejevo, once one of the most exciting, thriving cities in the world, was united under Federation control. Even more important, with the contending military forces separated and monitored by the peacekeeping force, the war was ended. In plain terms, this went far beyond anything foreign relations observers thought possible. Nevertheless, some aspects of the negotiations made the progress uncertain. Even though the Serbs, including Karadzic, signed the Dayton Accords, they did so under duress. It was no secret that extremist factions would move to undermine the newly agreed upon political accords, moving for a partitioning of Bosnia-Herzegovina in order to hold on to some fragment of power. On this subject Albright was adamant. "This first goal of the US must be to stop the war," she said, knowing that the fighting had to cease before the vast array of territorial issues that caused the conflict could be addressed. With this in mind, Albright made it clear to all concerned that no proposal would be considered that would permanently divide the region. On this, the President, Vice President, Secretary of State Christopher, General Shalikashvili, Richard

Holbrooke, and Albright were all in agreement. Quite simply, there would be no partitioning of Bosnia.

One key issue that was often overlooked by commentators, but not by Albright, was that for the cease-fire to hold, Bosnia, as a country, had to function as a single economic and social unit. Clearly, Bosnia and Serbia could not survive economically unless they revitalized the long-established, integrated commercial infrastructure that existed until the outbreak of war. While Croatia is more economically viable because of its coastal location, it too must be integrated into the regional economic structure.

The tenets of the agreement reached in Dayton were finalized in the Paris Peace Accord signed in December 1995 by all parties to the conflict.

That same month, President Clinton, following the recommendations of his foreign policy team—especially UN Envoy Albright—and in the face of virulent opposition, announced one of the most controversial decisions of his tenure as commander in chief: To commit American troops to Bosnia in an effort to prevent further bloodshed and give the new peace accord a chance. Sending in US troops, the President told the nation in a televised address, would signal other countries that the US was not shirking its responsibilities as the world's most powerful nation. We would not be committing troops to fight a war, he continued, but to ensure lasting peace in Bosnia.

Opposition to such a risky move was understandable, given the dangers involved and the precarious nature of the terrain—Bosnia is considered by many military experts to be among the most geographically perilous regions in

Europe. Nevertheless, President Clinton went forward with the deployment of 20,000 troops with one proviso: all US forces, while serving as part of the UN peacekeeping force, would remain under US command at all times. In implementing the Dayton Accords, the NATO-led Implementation Force (IFOR) performed magnificently, keeping the peace while incurring no casualties from hostile action, an astonishing record that attests to the respect in which NATO is held by all parties and the skill with which the IFOR commanders carried out their military mission. Indeed, a single Bosnia, with two entities, the core of the Dayton Accords, was permanently cemented by IFOR's policing of the new country's first unified democratic elections, which took place on September 14, 1996.

In Bosnia today, the four-year-long slaughter has halted. Wanton death and destruction have been replaced by a calm in which Serbs, Muslims, and Croats can stand side by side, if somewhat cautiously, hawking their goods in the town square of the formerly war-torn city of Sarajevo. Children have returned to school, and residents are able to attend their houses of worship, whether it be a church, a synagogue, or a mosque, without fear of being attacked. Albright herself has assessed the progress, saying, "Although the full promise of Dayton is not yet fulfilled, much has changed during the past thirteen months. The fighting has stopped, peaceful elections have been held, and the framework for national democratic institutions has taken shape. Much of this is due to American leadership. Our plan now, in cooperation with our many partners, is to consolidate and build on those gains. Our strategy is to continue diminishing the need for an international military presence by establishing a stable military balance, improving judicial and legal institutions, helping more people return safely to their homes and seeing that more of those indicted as war criminals are arrested and prosecuted."

As a result of the efforts of the Clinton administration's foreign policy team, of which Albright was an integral player, there is more than a ray of hope in the war-torn region. Today, in Bosnia, virtually every nation in Europe is working together to bring stability to a region where conflict earlier this century tore the continent apart. As the ambassador put it, "This reflects a sharp departure from the spheres of influence or balance of power diplomacy of the past, and an explicit rejection of politics based on ethnic identification. . . . As for IFOR, currently soldiers from NATO, Russia, Poland, Ukraine, Romania and many other nations trust, defend and depend on each other."

For all of the good work and diplomatic success by Madeleine Albright, Warren Christopher, and Richard Holbrooke in the Balkans, the Bosnian Peace Accord might never have happened had one major political figure had his way. Amazingly, the spoiler was not some spokesman for the ultra-right-wing isolationist wing of the Republican Party. Rather it was the hero of the Gulf War and the author of the quintessential doctrine on modern warfare, Chairman of the Joint Chiefs of Staff, General Colin Powell. Ironical, and even more amazing, was the fact that any kind of feud, public or private, with someone of Colin Powell's stature could ever be a positive thing.

The fact was, during the last year of his term as chairman, Powell took Albright on publicly, not only attacking her theory of assertive multilateralism, but opposing her on both Somalia and Bosnia, and generally, doing everything in his power to make Ambassador Albright a nonentity in the formulation of American foreign policy. For months the debate raged on in the press, editorial pages, network news shows, and the familiar hangouts of Washington's intelligentsia. As for the White House, many were skittish about any member of their foreign policy team taking on someone with Powell's stature and poll numbers. For Albright, it was not enough to focus her energies on a single country or particular issue. Even though she was supposed to be the top US diplomat to the rest of the world, at home Albright often found it necessary to draw on her skills as a negotiator to navigate a virtual minefield of detractors in the Powell camp on a host of controversial subjects ranging from land-mine decommissioning to Rwanda, not to mention the ongoing slaughter in the former Yugoslavia.

In his memoir, *My American Journey*, Joint Chiefs Chairman Powell recounts a debate in the early months of the Clinton administration with Ambassador Albright over the deployment of US troops in Bosnia, as part of an overall United Nations initiative to stop the civil war. "My constant unwelcome message at all of the meetings on Bosnia was simply that we would not commit military forces unless we had a clear political objective." To hear Powell tell it, Albright responded by querying, "What's the point of having this superb military that you're always talking about if we can't use it?"

By most accounts, Powell completely lost it, although the version in his memoir is far more self-serving. According to the General, he told Albright in no uncertain terms, "American GIs were not toy soldiers to be moved around on some sort of global game board. I patiently explained that we had used our armed forces more than two dozen times in the preceding three years for war, peacekeeping, disaster relief, and humanitarian assistance. But in every one of those cases we had a clear goal and had matched our military commitment to the goal. As a result, we had been successful in every case." He goes on, "I told Ambassador Albright that the US military would carry out any mission it was handed, but my advice would always be that tough political goals had to be set first." While this may have been the way the general remembered the exchange, few others did. It was common knowledge that Powell had virtually no patience with Albright's way of approaching a problem. In fact, he had little regard at all for the manner in which the Clinton administration formulated foreign policy. Powell, who opposed the use of air power in Bosnia, left the administration in late 1993 and, with some disdain, recalls the Clinton foreign policy–making machine as resembling a "graduate student bull session."

In all likelihood, the reason for the General's bitterness toward the Clinton White House, particularly its foreign policy team, stems not from a mere disagreement over tactics, but rather from the fact that many in the new administration viewed the much-heralded Powell Doctrine—that the US should intervene militarily and with overwhelming force, but only when vital American interests are threatened—as essentially obsolete, a Cold War relic.

As for Powell's condescending remarks comparing Albright's view of troop mobilization to a "global board game," she responded, "It's all a little patronizing. The fact is that Colin Powell is more than just a little wrong on Bosnia." Ironically, the same week his long-anticipated autobiography came out, NATO began air strikes against Bosnian Serb targets—air strikes that Powell had vehemently opposed. Albright, who had been the object of the general's wrath for months, particularly enjoyed the fact that the air strikes worked, playing a key role in driving the Bosnian Serbs to the negotiating table. In fact, the Bosnian Serbs' sudden accommodation stemmed, in the words of Albright, from "air power, combined with the success of the Croatian military offensive, division in the Bosnian Serb leadership, and the world's horror at the attacks on Sarajevo and Srebrenica," all of which "helped force the rival factions to the negotiating table in both Belgrade and Geneva."

For months, the debate between the two raged on. As Powell continued to second-guess her every move, the ambassador tried to put it in perspective. "The fact is, Colin Powell has a different approach to the use of power. I mean, of course you can use power when the earth is flat and you have six months to prepare and you're facing a crazy dictator with nuclear weapons and someone else is paying for it. But that is not always the situation." And as the administration's ultimate decision to commit to a military option was successful in bringing a halt to the ethnic violence, Albright has said, "I felt some vindication. . . . It wasn't easy being a civilian woman having a major disagreement with the hero of the Western world."

It was precisely that sort of comment, whether made at a principals' meeting, during a question and answer session after a speech, or during an appearance on the Sunday morning news shows, that, in the words of longtime Powell aides, "simply made the general nuts." Remarked one senior National Security Council official, "I've been at this job a long time and I've known Colin Powell for twenty years, and I've never seen anybody get under his skin as badly as Madeleine." Powell himself characterized one altercation with Albright as upsetting him so much that he "nearly had an aneurysm."

The feud grew uglier and more personal, culminating in a hostile exchange between Albright and Powell at Washington's annual Gridiron Dinner. There, amid an exclusive black-tie crowd of the capital's power set, Colin Powell was far from the charming, conciliatory model of patience he professed to be in *My American Journey*. Rather, as the two revisited his "American GIs are not toy soldiers" comment, it appeared to bystanders that, without meaning to, the general was questioning Albright's commitment to American troops.

To Albright, who had been born in the years before World War II, whose family had escaped both the Nazis and the Communists, immigrated to the United States as refugees, and been classified as displaced persons, Powell's characterization of her position was as inaccurate as his hostility was unwarranted. As for his "toy soldiers" comment, she has stated, "It's not true. I have the highest respect for the US military. They are very precious to me, as they are to every American and every policy maker. My concept is that the major role for the US military is obviously to defend and protect US national interests." As for the so-called Powell Doctrine, she says, "There are times when, according to very strict criteria, our use of our military in combination with our diplomacy is important for US national interests. I believe that, with very careful determination of what the criteria are, we should be able to use force when it helps our interests. I do think that there are times when under the proper constraints it's appropriate to use military force in some way other than massive overwhelming force."

As resolution of the Bosnian conflict continued to make progress—first with the UN-negotiated cease-fire, then with the Dayton Accords, and finally with the Paris Peace Treaty—it became overwhelmingly clear that the policies developed by Albright, Christopher, and the rest of the Clinton foreign policy team had taken the day. For Colin Powell, the hero of the Gulf War, working with the Clinton White House was never a good fit. As the consummate military professional, he came from a world of orderly, efficiently managed strategy meetings, and he expected no less from his peers. The new, young, and more liberal Clintonites embraced a free-form, almost academic method of problem solving. It was often time-consuming and inefficient. Yet it occasionally yielded extraordinary results, such as the American lead in restoring democracy to the war-torn island of Haiti. But in this context Colin Powell was odd man out. While the President respected him tremendously, there was simply no percentage for Powell in joining the team. Albright, for her part, seemed at first glance to offer a convenient target for attacks on the foreign policy of the new administration. As UN ambassador, she was officially on the periphery. Powell could weigh in with criticism to placate his legion of conservative supporters, yet avoid direct attacks on or criticism of the President. But as it turned out, Madeleine Albright was not comfortable playing the role of victim. Much to Powell's surprise, not only did Albright fail to back down, but she was lying in wait, ready for his attack.

The bottom line was that, in grossly underestimating Albright, Colin Powell overlooked one major factor. Contrary to the assumptions of many, the ambassador was not some vulnerable diplomat outside the decision-making loop. To those who knew her, the reason was obvious: Madeleine Albright was raised by such a diplomat—her father, Josef Korbel—who had very nearly lost his life by being vulnerable and out of the loop. Powell somehow seemed ignorant of the fact that Albright had been basically raised at her father's knee, growing up hearing him speak of his days as a rising star in the Czech diplomatic corps. Albright has spoken of the times when her father would reminisce, saying how unexpected the Communist takeover of Czechoslovakia had been, how, being stationed in Pakistan at the time, he had no way of knowing that a coup was in the offing and that virtually no one was watching his back. It was a painful lesson that very nearly cost Josef Korbel his life, for he was sentenced to death in absentia by the coup plotters.

Suffice it to say, from the day Madeleine Albright accepted President Clinton's appointment as ambassador to the UN she understood the vulnerability of her position. She was well aware that she was facing four years of walking through a professional minefield, that as long as she was stationed in New York, her rear flank in Washington was exposed. Fortunately, it was during this time that years of reciprocal loyalty with such players as Warren Christopher and Sandy Berger really paid off. What's more, Albright's close friendship with General John Shalikashvili, the vice chairman to Powell on the Joint Chiefs of Staff during the first two years of the administration, proved invaluable. In short, any attempt by Powell to isolate Ambassador Albright or freeze her out was doomed from the start. In fact, she won a battle of wills with her detractors by taking on the biggest, toughest guy in the neighborhood, the guy everybody else was afraid to challenge.

In one respect, Colin Powell did Albright something of a favor. As it happened, despite her solid power base as the most powerful American UN envoy in history, Albright, like any other cabinet-level official, still needed an issue by which to define her term in office. Ironically, by going on the offensive, General Colin Powell gave her exactly what she needed. Up to this point, no administration official had been in a position to challenge the hero of the Gulf War, and Powell knew it. Operating with a kind of public relations immunity, he could comment on virtually any issue, saying anything at any time, without fear of retaliation. He could support the President one day and attack him the next, and get away with it. All this changed the day that General Powell decided to take on Madeleine Albright. It didn't happen overnight, but over a matter of months. Little by little, as the tide turned in Bosnia, Albright's star began to rise and the Powell Doctrine, despite all the book sales, became just another chapter in the history of American foreign policy. Unfortunately for General Powell, he forgot one of the basic rules of surviving in the nation's capital: *in Washington, if you are going to pick a fight, make sure you can win.*

As Albright has said, the success of the administration's policy to restore peace in the Balkans has brought her and the rest of the Clinton foreign policy team some measure of vindication. But more than vindication, the consistent opposition by Republicans in Congress and detractors such as General Powell, served as a catalyst, motivating her to do more than simply find a means of stopping the bloody conflict in Bosnia. And while she never considered the General's constant derision and belittling of her position as a personal affront, she was determined to take on an even greater challenge that in every respect, was completely personal. As a child of the Holocaust, Madeleine Albright understood the politics of genocide perhaps better than anyone in the diplomatic community. For her it wasn't enough simply to achieve a cease-fire via the Dayton Accords. The reality was that there were brutal, diabolical men roaming free in the Bosnian countryside. Men, who not unlike their predecessors in the Nazi SS and Gestapo, had ordered the mass rape and slaughter of thousands of noncombatants. As incredible as it seemed, these modern-day leaders were the architects of organized mass murder in the year 1995. In her heart, Albright knew there could be no true peace in Bosnia unless these war criminals were brought to justice. Therefore, shortly after the warring parties went to the negotiating table for the first time, she took the lead in officially calling for the formation of an international war crimes tribunal. For Madeleine Albright, this was personal. Very personal.

The image is itself chilling: a young man and his wife, their twenty-two-month-old daughter in his arms, wrapped in a blanket to fend off the cold dampness of winter. It is midnight in downtown Prague, well past curfew. For several hours they have walked the streets, ducking in and out of cafés hoping not to be recognized, as well as alleys or any other dark place they could find. Half a dozen times, as they crouched in the shadows, they could hear the Nazi patrols passing within a few feet of them. The patrols, usually made up of three or four armed soldiers, tipped off their prey by the sound of the steel heels of their spit-and-polish marching boots. First came the unmistakable clicking noise. Then the sound of profanity-laced conversation in German, barely audible at first. Seconds passed as the voices grew louder and louder until the soldiers were almost upon Josef and Anna Korbel and their baby daughter, Madeleine Jana. Their hearts raced as they had no way of knowing if they were about to be discovered. Would a sudden movement give them away? Would tiny Madeleine awaken and suddenly begin to cry revealing their whereabouts?

That night the Korbel family had good reason to be afraid. As a diplomat, Josef Korbel, like many in his country's foreign service, had been put on a death list only days after the Nazi invasion. If discovered, he would be summarily executed in the street and his wife and child would inevitably be sent to the death camps. Still, they were luckier than most as Josef was able to use his connections to obtain fake diplomatic papers that would allow him and his young family to cross the border and escape occupied Czechoslovakia. Unfortunately, the papers would not be ready for several days, and knowing that to return home would mean certain death, they had no choice but to disappear into the night. Somehow, the Korbels were able to remain hidden as the soldiers passed this time. And, for the next several days the terrifying encounter would repeat itself over and over again until the papers arrived. Miraculously, the family escaped occupied Prague and made their way to London, where they rode out the war. At the time, young Madeleine Jana Korbel had no way of knowing it, but she was experiencing the first real defining moment of her life. As her parents risked their lives to save hers, she embarked not on a life on the run, but rather the first leg of an incredible journey to the place of her destiny. A place called America.

Albright was born on May 15, 1937, in Prague,

Czechoslovakia. She has one sister, Anna, and a brother, John, who were born some years later. Her father was a member of the Czech diplomatic service, and between 1937 and 1948 the Korbel family lived in Belgrade, London, Prague, and then again in Belgrade. By all accounts Albright adjusted well to the constant change in scenery. "I made friends very easily. I think it has to do with the fact that I lived in a lot of different countries, went to a lot of different schools, and was always being put into situations where I had to relate to the people around me." By her own admission, she gained her early diplomatic training at her father's knee, as he often enlisted her to present bouquets to visiting dignitaries during welcoming ceremonies. While in London, English became Albright's first second language. By the time her father had his second posting in Belgrade, this time as ambassador, she was being tutored exclusively by governesses. This stemmed from the fact that her father, who was staunchly opposed to totalitarianism, held a profound fear that by letting his daughter attend the local schools, she would come under the influence of the Communists. By age ten, he avoided the problem once and for all by sending her to an exclusive boarding school in Switzerland.

In 1948, Josef Korbel was posted at the United Nations Commission for India and Pakistan, and he relocated to Bombay. Shortly thereafter, the Czech government was overthrown in a Communist coup that charged him with crimes against the state. For the second time in ten years Josef Korbel was sentenced to death by a dictatorship. Moving quickly, he applied for and was granted political asylum in the US for himself and his family, as the State Department classified the Korbels as displaced persons.

Along the way, Albright and her family underwent the sudden and painful transition from one of Prague's finest families to mere refugees. As one friend of Albright explained it, "Picture your life. Your job, your friends, your house, the school that your children attend, and the playground on which they play. One day it's there and everything is wonderful. And the next day, tanks from a German Special Army Panzer Division are rolling down the streets and Nazi storm troopers begin to round up your friends, your coworkers, your family. In a matter of days everything you own and care about is taken from you. And on top of that, a battalion of the best trained soldiers in the world are hunting you down, trying to kill you. As amazing as it sounds, that was Madeleine Albright's life as a little girl."

As Albright tells it, "I remember spending huge portions of my life in air-raid shelters, singing songs with my father and mother. I remember when we moved to Walton-on-Thames, when they had just invented some kind of a steel table. They said if our house was bombed and you were under the table, you would survive. We had this table, and we ate on the table and we slept under the table and we played around the table." Few who have heard this story have failed to appreciate its impact on Madeleine Albright. "She watched her world fall apart, and ever since, she has dedicated her life to spreading to the rest of the world the freedom and tolerance her family found here in America," said President Bill Clinton.

Between the sound of the air-raid sirens signaling the nightly blitzkrieg of London by the German Luftwaffe, struggling to find enough food to eat on the streets of the war-ravaged city, and not knowing when and if her family could ever return to their homeland, Madeleine Albright's worldview was defined at an early age. Couple that with the fact that she was extremely close to her father who, being a foreign service officer, was privy to all the officially denied rumors of mass genocide taking place throughout the European theater, and it is no surprise that Albright will always have the heart and soul of a refugee. "My life and my parents' life was a reflection of the turbulence of the twentieth century. I had this feeling that there but for the grace of God, we might have been dead." In some respects, Madeleine Albright's rather Wilsonian view that the formation of a Bosnian war crimes tribunal was imperative to the peace process, is a living tribute to her parents. The Wilsonians argue that lasting peace must be built upon reconciliation, and that means justice. For the 250,000 dead as a result of the Bosnian civil war, many of whom were victims of ethnic cleansing by the rival factions, justice can only mean uncovering the truth about exactly what happened and bringing the guilty, whether they be Serbs, Croats, or others to justice. "I care about issues of genocide and persecution. I care because of the way I was brought up by my parents," says Albright. "What they gave us children was the gift of life, literally. Twice, once by giving us birth and the other by bringing us to America to escape what clearly now would have been a certain death."

For a number of years, however, Albright and the Wilsonian view on the formation of a war crimes tribunal faced opposition from almost every quarter. Some in the General Assembly felt it was a weak substitute for a stronger international initiative in the Balkans. Others suggested that it was a guilt-driven response, "too little too late," by the United Nations for its failure to intervene earlier to stop the killing in Bosnia. Predictably, France was reluctant to lend its support, in part because the world's lone superpower, the US, backed it, and partly because they held the view that it would somehow be unfair to single out the former Yugoslavia, while such perpetrators of mass killings as Pol Pot and Saddam Hussein go uncharged. Unexpectedly, Great Britain, America's most consistent ally in international security matters, opposed the formation of the tribunal for more practical considerations such as the fact that unlike Nuremberg, in which the Allies were trying the surrendered leaders of a defeated nation, most of the major war criminals in Bosnia—specifically, Serbian President Slobodan Milosevic, Bosnian Serb military leader Ratko Mladic and political strongman Radovan Karadzic—were not even in custody. That, along with nagging issues such as the unavailability or intimidation of witnesses and the difficulty of obtaining access to evidence, especially to the mass graves in regions under Serb control, made the prospect of launching a war crimes tribunal all the more daunting.

Nevertheless, Albright was unrelenting in her cause, citing incomprehensible acts of cruelty, including stories of purposeful humiliation of prisoners, sexual sadism, genital mutilation, and the forcing of prisoners to copulate at gunpoint. Sources confirm that those who failed to submit were beaten to death with sledgehammers, tire irons, and rifle butts. According to Albright in a major address on the subject, "The magnitude of the war crimes committed in the former Yugoslavia demands an international legal response. The war itself is the result of premeditated, armed aggression. Bosnian Serb leaders have sought a final solution of extermination or expulsion to the problem of non-Serb populations under their control. The means chosen include murder, torture, indiscriminate bombing, fire, dismemberment, rape, and castration. Half of Bosnia's population has been displaced. Five percent have been killed. Abuses have been massive, repeated, deliberate and gross. And no side is without guilt."

As to France's complaint that the players in the former Yugoslavia are somehow being singled out while perpetrators of similar violence in other conflicts have never been pursued, the UN ambassador was equally blunt. "It is the position of the United States that simply because some war crimes may go unpunished that does not mean that they should all go unpunished. We oppose any sort of amnesty for the architects of ethnic cleansing." As for the British concerns about the inherent forensic obstacles to the success of the tribunal, she responded, "We do not believe that the difficulty of the tribunal's work should bar the attempt." Finally, after months of public maneuvering and back-channel negotiation, Albright was able to persuade the other representatives on the UN Security Council to back a resolution calling for the formation of a Bosnian war crimes tribunal. It was formally established in May

1993 with a start-up budget of $11 million. Additionally, the US Congress put its money where Albright's mouth was, making a special voluntary contribution of $3 million and authorizing the President to provide up to $25 million in goods and services to the tribunal.

On December 14, 1995, the Paris Peace Treaty, based on the tenets of the Dayton Accords, was signed by the leaders of the warring factions. Finally, President Clinton, Warren Christopher, Richard Holbrooke, and Madeleine Albright saw the fruit of their years of labor in the Balkans. But for Albright, there was a special satisfaction in knowing that, in order to secure the peace treaty, the US had not backed off its commitment to the War Crimes Tribunal. She knew that, as the principals each signed the document, the voices of the 250,000 victims of the Bosnian civil war would not go unheard. Her commitment to remembrance and vindication of the victims of the war was eloquently demonstrated during a speech at the US Holocaust Museum in Washington when she reflected on a recent trip to Bosnia. There, before a packed auditorium, Albright recalled images of "streams of refugees expelled from their homes in and around Vukovar. The images were eerily familiar. They could have come right out of the pictures in this museum of families fleeing Warsaw or Minsk or Bucharest or Prague. The faces were not the same, but the expressions and the moments were—the slow, stumbling, bewildered pace of uprooted families, burdened by their only remaining possessions, trudging down an unfamiliar road toward an uncertain future, the strong helping the weak until their own strength drained." Most of the victims, she continued, "were men and women like you and me—boys and girls like those we know—intentionally targeted not because of what they had done, but for who they were."

Ambassador Albright paused for a moment and gazed into the audience, many of whom had tears running down their faces. She wanted them to hear the message. She wanted them to get the analogy. For at that moment, they were no longer listening to UN Ambassador Albright talking foreign policy. They were hearing a terrified eight-year-old girl named Madeleine Jana, a refugee, speaking from the heart.

7

NOT EXACTLY
A MAN'S WORLD

The United Nations Conference

on Women in Beijing and the

"No *Cojónes*" Speech

Madeleine Albright meets with French Foreign Minister Hervé de Charette. AGENCE FRANCE PRESSE/CORBIS-BETTMANN

Madeleine Albright plants a tree in the garden of the U.S. Embassy, in memory of the late U.S. Ambassador to France, Pamela Harriman. AGENCE FRANCE PRESSE/CORBIS-BETTMANN

Madeleine Albright shakes hands with her Japanese counterpart, Yukihiko Ikeda, prior to their talks.
AGENCE FRANCE PRESSE/CORBIS-BETTMANN

Japanese Prime Minister Ryutaro Hashimoto shakes hands with Madeleine Albright. AGENCE FRANCE PRESSE/CORBIS-BETTMANN

Secretary of State Albright and U.S. Joint Chiefs of Staff Chairman General John Shalikashvili.

AGENCE FRANCE PRESSE/CORBIS-BETTMANN

Secretary of State Albright announces U.S. sanctions on Burma.

Madeleine Albright speaks with National Security Advisor Sandy Berger. AGENCE FRANCE PRESSE/CORBIS-BETTMANN

Madeleine Albright blows out candles on her birthday cake.
AGENCE FRANCE PRESSE/CORBIS-BETTMANN

Madeleine Albright testifies before the Senate Finance Committee as U.S. Trade Representative Charlene Barshefsky looks on. AGENCE FRANCE PRESSE/CORBIS-BETTMANN

Madeleine Albright talks to reporters before a U.N. Security Council meeting. REUTERS/CORBIS-BETTMANN

Madeleine Albright at the U.N. Security Council in New York.
REUTERS/CORBIS-BETTMANN

At the U.N. General Assembly, Madeleine Albright replies to a speech by Iraq's Deputy Prime Minister Tareq Aziz on October 7, 1994, as Iraqi troops mass on the Kuwaiti border.
REUTERS/CORBIS-BETTMANN

Secretary of State–designate Madeleine Albright during her confirmation hearings before the Senate Foreign Relations Committee. AGENCE FRANCE PRESSE/CORBIS-BETTMANN

There are three things that really irk people close to Madeleine Albright. The first is that when she talks tough, the media instinctively ascribes a butch quality to her comments. The second is when so-called highly placed diplomatic officials, speaking, predictably on the condition of anonymity, describe the Secretary of State as an intellectual lightweight. Third, and by all accounts the most preposterous, is the suggestion that she attended the 1995 United Nations Conference on Women in Beijing as an afterthought. As anyone who knows Madeleine Albright well will tell you, the new Secretary of State never, ever, does anything as an afterthought.

Far from being an afterthought, then-Ambassador Albright's attendance at the Women's Summit was a topic of highly contentious, emotionally charged debate both within the administration and on Capitol Hill. Opposition to US participation in the Conference rang in from all quarters, both in this country and abroad. Ironically, the loudest and most outspoken attacks came from forces on the extreme elements of the political spectrum. On the ultraright, pro-life forces, who saw the Conference as a worldwide forum to promote birth control and abortion, mounted a well-financed, grassroots opposition campaign, the likes of which had not been seen in Washington since the massive effort to discredit Anita Hill during the confirmation hearings for Justice Clarence Thomas several years ago. On the left, a coalition of human-rights groups, including activists from two dozen countries, attempted a similar effort to stop Albright's participation, but instead, spent most of its money on a costly media campaign. The slick, hard-hitting attack ads, ran for weeks throughout the summer, highlighting the People's Republic's horrendous record on human rights, citing Tiananmen Square and the incarceration of human rights activist Harry Wu as prime examples. Both factions demanded that there be no high-level participation in the Conference, with the pro-life groups insisting that there be no participation in the summit by the United States whatsoever.

For Madeleine Albright, it was not enough that the US simply make an appearance in Beijing. As the "indispensable nation," as she is fond of calling it, it was vital that the US assume a visible leadership role in the Conference.

Notwithstanding the human-rights record of the Chinese or the objections of the pro-life movement, Albright was resolute in her belief that the international community was entering a critical phase. A phase that, absent the ever-present danger of the Cold War, afforded a brief window of opportunity for the nations of the world to include a segment of its population that had been traditionally excluded from the development of foreign policy. Plainly, Albright saw a chance to include the treatment of women—who, in many parts of the world are born into lives of virtual servitude and exploitation—as a priority, a top agenda item in deciding what country gets foreign aid and which does not, who gets sophisticated weaponry and F-16s and who does not.

Her position was clear. "Despite recent gains, women remain an undervalued and underdeveloped human resource. In many societies—especially in rural, agriculturally based areas—they do the vast majority of the work. But they do not own the land; they are not taught to read; they cannot obtain personal or business loans; and they are denied equal access to the levers of political decision making." The ambassador made certain to point out that the indignities to which women are subjected are more than just economic. "In Angola, one-third of all homicides are perpetrated against women, usually by their husbands. In Thailand, child prostitution is growing because clients believe older prostitutes are more likely to be infected by HIV." And in some parts of the world, "there is the despicable notion that rape is just another tactic of war," she had said. No, it was clear in the summer of 1995, that

Albright saw a chance to redefine the terms of the foreign policy debate, to determine what was on the table and what was not, to actually mandate that the human rights of women become an inexorable part of the international landscape. She also saw that the Beijing Conference was a critical step in pursuing this goal and that there might not be a second chance. With that in mind, Albright mounted a campaign of her own.

For Albright and the White House, the timing could hardly have been worse. When the controversy over US participation in the Conference first began to heat up, in June of 1995, the President's poll numbers were still floundering just under the 50 percent mark. While progress was being made on a number of issues by the White House, most inhabitants of the West Wing during that time agreed that they were in for a long, hot summer. Despite the fact that in every region of the country the economy appeared to be flourishing, other issues on the domestic front—notably, the Whitewater investigation, the lack of a budget deal, and an increasingly uncooperative Republican congress—continued to gnaw at the administration. On top of all this, significant foreign policy matters had yet to be resolved or were still in the implementation phase in places such as Bosnia and Rwanda, and of course, the Middle East. At the time, virtually no one would have predicted Bill Clinton's reelection, let alone his decisive victory over Bob Dole eighteen months later.

Although Ambassador Albright had no intention of retreating from her stance on US attendance at Beijing, she nevertheless was mindful that any mishandling of the matter ran the risk of turning the Conference as well as her own involvement in it, into a major campaign issue. In other words, a cabinet official's worst nightmare.

Acutely aware of the risk to her and her boss, Albright approached the challenge of the Beijing Conference with the calm of a bomb squad technician, using surgical precision in her every move. First, she carefully assessed the situation, determining where in fact the opposition camps were actually positioned. If her effort was to be successful, she could not afford to overlook anything, to misconstrue official loyalty with loyalty in fact. Domestically, the pro-life and human-rights groups had been obvious. More subtle were niche groups supporting Taiwan and the Dalai Lama. Moreover, the usual resistance from conservative members of Congress came as no surprise, since they opposed 90 percent of what the UN did anyway. Somewhat surprisingly, another pocket of opposition that was beginning to emerge was the fledgling Republican presidential primary committees that were gearing up for the nomination fight. The biggest and best financed was the Phil Gramm campaign. Gramm, a conservative senator from Texas, was touted as the early front-runner for the GOP nomination, and was running on a platform of family values and a balanced budget. The others, Lamar Alexander, Dick Lugar, Alan Keyes, and millionaire publishing heir Steve Forbes, all opposed the Conference to one degree or another, as did Senator Bob Dole. This made for a rather interesting dynamic. Given that all of these candidates were vying for the Republican nomination and they all agreed with each other on the Women's Conference, each campaign organization spent exhaustive amounts of time and resources trying to appear to be the candidate that disagreed the most with Bill Clinton. Although it was early in the process, during one informal candidates' forum, one tongue-tied Republican attempted in vain to put his opposition to the summit in context. "Senator," he began. "I strongly denounce the Women's Conference in Communist China. And it's not that I disagree with your position. It's just that I disagree with Bill and Hillary Clinton's position on the summit more than you do." And so it went throughout the summer as the numerous campaign organizations went on the offensive, firing barbs at the President and First Lady that ranged from the relatively mild charge that they were cozying up to human-rights violators to the more extreme charge that the Conference was merely a front to internationally endorse lesbian marriage and governmentally mandated quotas for childbearing. Given the arcane nature of the Republican attacks, Albright was not particularly concerned, so long as the thinking inside the White House remained unaffected. On that subject, however, the jury was still out as late as mid-July.

To Albright's dismay, there was a considerable amount of disagreement inside the White House on the pros and cons of a high-profile presence of the American government at the Beijing Conference. Ironically, much of it emanated from some of the same White House officials who made up the Corporate Board that would seek to deny Albright the post of Secretary of State two years later. Much of the skittishness stemmed from the concern that the Republican opposition to the Conference, led by Newt

Gingrich in the House and by Jesse Helms in the Senate, was so intense that funding and support for other critical international initiatives such as Bosnia would be held hostage. Albright, for her part, was unimpressed, commenting that past administrations had used the Cold War as an excuse to avoid addressing the issue of human rights for women for four decades. "After Bosnia, what will it be next, an attack from outer space?" she was heard to say.

Opponents inside the West Wing pointed out that there was significant opposition to the Beijing Conference in general, much of it coming from outside the United States. To some extent they had a point, as most analysts agree that the battle lines on the issue of women's rights were first drawn at the 1993 Human Rights Conference in Vienna and later at the World Population Conference in Cairo in 1994. And, while Vice President Al Gore, as the head of the American delegation in Cairo, was able to achieve significant gains there, reaching compromise language on abortion, many of the same hard-line antagonists at both conventions had regrouped and reorganized to oppose any similar initiatives that might happen at Beijing. Islamic countries such as Iran and the Sudan strongly opposed proposed conference language that defined women's rights as an "indivisible part of universal human rights." And in a surprising twist, they had a strange bedfellow in the Vatican, which as a matter of course opposes recognition of sexual and reproductive rights. During one strategy session, an extremely agitated staffer in the White House political shop made it clear that the Catholic Church—whose sudden withdrawal of support proved to be a fatal blow to the administration's Health Care Reform Bill—meant business, by planning to send a highly respected Harvard law professor, Mary Ann Glendon, as its chief delegate. For her part, Albright was well aware of the Vatican's aggressive stance, knowing that it had intended all along not only to challenge the Cairo language, but to turn the clock back, calling for the elimination of basic tenets agreed to at the last Women's Conference in Nairobi ten years earlier. All the more reason for a high-profile US presence, she maintained, pointing out that a legion of powerful women had committed to attend the Conference, including three prime ministers, a president, three queens, and many other senior government officials. With that comment, Madeleine Albright showed her hand, revealing for the first time what her true aim was: the attendance of the UN Conference on Women by the First Lady.

By August the public position of the administration was that the US would attend and participate in the Summit, but the composition of the delegation was still being worked out. While this and the idea of Hillary Clinton's participation were debated internally at the White House, Albright took her case to the public, delivering numerous speeches on the subject. During one memorable speech before her old think tank, the Center for National Policy, Albright, in typical fashion, called it as she saw it. "The fourth World Conference on Women will convene in China in thirty-three days and, let there be no doubt, the United States will be there." She went on to say that the administration would "use the Conference in Beijing to underline the truth that violence against women is no one's prerogative; it is not a cultural choice; it is not an inevitable consequence of biology—it is a crime that we all have a responsibility to condemn, prevent, punish, and stop." In response to a suggestion that the US should withdraw from the Conference because of China's human rights record, Albright did not miss a beat. "The suggestion is well motivated, but misses the main point. American withdrawal would not stop the Conference or cause it to be moved; it would lead instead to a Conference in which 130 million American women would be unrepresented and in which American influence and leadership would not be felt."

All along it had been Albright's position that it made no sense to boycott a conference on the grounds of human rights when the conference had as its primary purpose the promotion of human rights. Finally, on the controversial subject of Harry Wu, the imprisoned Chinese-American human rights activist, the UN envoy pulled no punches, "He should be released immediately and unharmed." However, Albright, was also aware of sensitive, behind-the-scenes negotiations that were taking place to secure Wu's release. Bearing that in mind, as well as the fact that embarrassing the Chinese government at this critical stage minimized the significance of the issue, she told her audience that in her view, there was "no real relationship" between US Conference attendance and Wu's release. Finally, she pointed out that the Chinese would have been just as happy if the US stayed home, thereby drawing less attention to the issue of women's rights in the host country. What Albright did not tell her audience that day was that while the Chinese were indifferent to US participation in the Conference, they very much did not want the world's only superpower to stay away because of Harry Wu.

As the September deadline for a decision approached some progress had been made. It was agreed that the US would send a high-level delegation and that UN Ambassador Albright would be the head of the delegation pending a decision on the attendance of the First Lady. The clock was ticking, yet two issues continued to hold up a decision. One was of course, Harry Wu, who the Chinese had announced was now about to go on trial for espionage just at the time the Conference was to begin. Mrs. Clinton, in fact, received a letter from Wu's wife, begging her not to attend. As if that was not enough, a second issue surfaced, this one involving Beijing's treatment of the many Non-Governmental Organizations—interest groups and associations—that sought to attend the Conference. The official Chinese policy was that such entities, which included delegations on behalf of Tibetan women and Taiwanese groups, would not be permitted to get anywhere near the site of the official UN Conference, instead being exiled to the obscure, rain-soaked town of Huairou, ninety minutes outside of Beijing. "China couldn't have handled this more poorly," said Undersecretary of State Tim Wirth. "On issue after issue, they seemed to be thumbing their noses at the international community."

In Albright's view, the issue of the NGO's could be handled, if not perfectly, at least practically. First, she explained to the First Lady and her staff that there was nothing the US could do for the thousands of women and groups that would be unable to get visas to attend the conference—Jane Fonda and Sally Field were two notable applicants who were rejected—but there was nothing stopping both her and the First Lady from making an appearance at Huairou. Generally, this proposal was met with a positive reaction, especially by Mrs. Clinton. "Finally, the plan is coming together," commented Albright to a colleague.

Nothing happened for several days as the State Department continued to monitor the Harry Wu situation. With the President and the First Lady on board, Albright was on the lookout for signs of trouble. She was well aware that the Corporate Board, minus the Vice President, who was 100 per cent behind the Conference, still was against sending a high-profile delegation and hated the idea of the First Lady going to Beijing, let alone Huairou. And then something unusual happened. A one-page memo was circulated among those in the foreign policy decision-making loop. It was unsigned, but many had strong suspicions as to the identity of the author.

The text of the memo read as follows:

Imagine that you live in a world in which you get to attend school about a third as long as everyone else. No homecoming, no prom, no graduation. Consider what it must be like, when you are only ten years old, to be carried into the village square and have friends of the family hold your legs open so that you are spread eagle, while a local midwife, at the direction of your maternal grandmother, uses a crude, filthy knife to perform an archaic mutilation of your genitals in the name of female purity. Imagine that, as a small child, you are sold into prostitution by your own parents. Imagine that you are five months pregnant and the government informs you that you have exceeded your quota of children. Imagine that a doctor from a government clinic forcibly performs an abortion on you, killing your child and then sterilizing you permanently. Imagine that you are planning your wedding, but your family is poor and cannot deliver the expected dowry to your fiancé's family. You and your family are disgraced. So are they. But instead of just being angry, they decide to kill you to void the marital contract.

Finally, imagine that you are not an American. Imagine that you are a woman.

And while no one in the White House or the State Department has ever claimed credit for the memo, several sources attest that its effects were felt up and down the halls of the West Wing. For once, geopolitical concerns were put on the back burner as those in the decision-making loop, even the Corporate Board began to look at the faces of the women affected by these Hunnish practices.

For whatever reason, a break came on the first of September when Beijing announced that it had sentenced Harry Wu to fifteen years in prison for espionage and then promptly put him on an Air China jetliner from Shanghai to the United States. When word came of his release the administration wasted no time. With the game of diplomatic chess over for now, the next day, the State Department announced that First Lady Hillary Clinton would indeed be leading the American delegation to the Women's Conference in Beijing, as its honorary chairperson. As for Albright, she was still the official head of the delegation and she deserved it. During a time when Democrats throughout the country were on the run, she saw the moral imperative staring her and the Clinton administration right square in the face. An opportunity to inject the cultural and institutional indignities endured by women into the forefront of public debate would not come along again for another ten years, until the next Women's Conference. Albright knew in her heart and her head that she had no choice but to seize the moment. So she did what she did best. She talked tough, real tough, not butch as her critics charge. As far as being an intellectual lightweight was concerned, the ambassador outmaneuvered dozens of the best political operators in Washington and the UN, not to mention Beijing. And finally, far from being an afterthought, she attended the UN Conference on Women, on her own terms, with a high-profile delegation, leading the charge alongside the First Lady.

So how did things go in Beijing? The big surprise was that despite the fact that the Chinese government did everything in its power to prevent its success, significant accomplishments were gained, and most reports indicated that the bulk of delegates in attendance actually enjoyed themselves. The First Lady's speech proclaiming that "women's rights are human rights" received a seemingly endless standing ovation, as did her address the following day at the NGO rally in Huairou. And Madeleine Albright, one of only six female ambassadors in attendance, literally brought the house down, with her speech to the NGO Conference interrupted by rousing cheers and applause so often that she was barely able to complete it. For Albright, who spends most of her time in a virtually all-male environment, it was a tremendous change of pace. "It was great," said the ambassador, as aides led her along a muddy walkway to her car. "In the UN it gets pretty lonely."

On a calm Saturday afternoon on February 24, 1996, three American civilian aircraft manned by members of a Florida-based anti-Castro group, "Brothers to the Rescue," departed a remote Florida airfield and headed for Cuba. The purpose of the flight was to drop, as they had on many previous missions, anti-Castro leaflets over the streets of downtown Havana. According to plan, one of the group's planes briefly entered Cuban airspace to drop its payload while the two others remained safely outside the prohibited zone. Or so they thought. While the third plane, having completed its mission, reversed its direction and zoomed past them in the direction of Florida, the pilots of the two escort aircraft attempted to follow suit. They never got the chance.

Even though every log, radar, and satellite reconnaissance photo confirms that the two civilian aircraft were unmistakably in international airspace, they were intercepted by a Cuban MIG 29 that had been authorized by a military control tower in Havana to attack. In seconds the two unarmed civilian aircraft were destroyed by air-to-air heat-seeking missiles, exploding in midair, killing both pilots and two passengers.

While the actions of the Cuban government were reprehensible, they was not nearly as callous as the conduct of the pilots of the Cuban fighter who, after killing four innocent people, could be overheard via short wave radio, gloating, shouting *"Arriba, Arriba,"* in an apparent fit of machismo at having shot down two unarmed civilian aircraft. By the time reports of the pilots' unconscionable reaction hit the airways, it served in further fueling anti-Castro feeling in this country and for lack of a better term, just pissed off a whole lot of Americans. One of those Americans was Madeleine Albright.

Weeks later, as the US formulated its response to the unprovoked attack by Castro's air force, UN Envoy Madeleine Albright made a campaign appearance with President Clinton before a Cuban-American rally in Miami's Orange Bowl. It was an overcast, breezy day for March, especially for south Florida. Nevertheless over 60,000 Cuban-Americans showed up, and most of them cheered wildly as Albright was introduced. For those who knew of her, they loved her tough talk, her unabashed patriotism, her love of America. They knew instinctively what one of her closest friends, former vice presidential candidate Geraldine Ferraro knew personally. "Madeleine is not easily threatened. If you messed with her on the street, she would probably get right in your face and tell you you are not worth fighting over. But don't ever bad-mouth the United

States in front of her. Believe me, no one attacks Madeleine's country and gets away with it."

Somehow, the standing-room-only crowd that day at the Orange Bowl could sense this about the diminutive ambassador. It was an election year and Florida, with its twenty-five electoral votes, was critical to the President's reelection. Moreover, the timing could not have been better for Albright to make an appearence, delivering a tough anti-Castro speech, particularly when Bob Dole had been crisscrossing the state, attacking President Clinton for being soft on Cuba. No, at the time, a little Castro-bashing would have been a huge help. But whatever they expected, nobody in the crowd was ready for what was about to come out of Madeleine Albright's mouth. In reference to the pilots of the Cuban MIGs that downed the unarmed Brothers to the Rescue aircraft, Albright went for the jugular. Staring into a sea of Cuban emigrés, people who, while they missed their homeland, truly loved this country, she shouted into the microphone, "Frankly, this is not *cojónes*, this is cowardice!"

At the time, the crowd was ecstatic, shouting in a chorus, "Madeleine, *libertad!* Madeleine, *libertad!*" The cheering was so intense that the rest of her speech was practically inaudible. So impressed was the President that he joked later, "We thought she was running for mayor of Miami down here." The Cuban-American crowd loved it so much that they had bumper stickers printed quoting the UN ambassador. Nevertheless, not everyone was pleased. Predictably, the reaction among her fellow delegates at the UN was reserved. "It was her worst move diplomatically," said one colleague. Another, Venezuelan Ambassador Diego Arria, said "She tried to say a man's word, and it was uncalled for. I wouldn't ever say that word, not even on my farm." Despite the sudden attack of civility and decorum among her colleagues in the General Assembly, the Orange Bowl speech was one of Madeleine Albright's truly great moments, combining some of her most powerful strengths—intuitiveness, toughness, and a tremendous sense of humor. Eric White, a prominent Washington lobbyist, may have put it best, saying, "On that day, Madeleine Albright uttered the mother of all sound bites."

Perhaps without meaning to, the ambassador may have given the President the public relations cover he needed to take action against Cuba. Prior to the speech public opinion was still divided over how to deal with the Havana government. Only days after her speech, which had been showcased on all the network news shows, leaders of both parties set aside partisan differences and hammered out a consensus version of a bill that became known as the Helms-Burton Bill, which President Clinton ultimately signed into law as the Cuban Liberty and Democratic Solidarity Act. Specifically, the act tightens the existing US embargo on Cuba by imposing additional economic sanctions on the Cuban regime. It also mandates the preparation of a plan for US assistance to a transitional and democratically elected Cuban government.

While Madeleine Albright's style may not suit every member of the General Assembly, it is fair to say that her very presence sufficiently changes the dynamic enough that her colleagues have begun to think twice about how to address many of the long-standing issues before the body. She is the first to admit that she is not everyone's cup of tea. But more often than not, Albright's direct, self-effacing manner and ability to take complex issues and boil them down so the average citizen can understand them, tends to be highly effective. Despite the criticism of her detractors on the Security Council, her tough, no-nonsense approach, tempered with the proper dose of humor, worked in the Orange Bowl that day, and would continue throughout her term as UN envoy. In all probability, this skill will translate into her role as Secretary of State. Said one admirer of Albright's at Foggy Bottom, "Finally, we have a Secretary with some *cojónes*."

8

TEST OF WILLS

The Power Struggle to Oust

Boutros Boutros-Ghali

Almost from the day of her arrival at the General Assembly as the US permanent representative to the UN, Ambassador Madeleine Albright and Secretary General Boutros Boutros-Ghali were headed for a showdown. Outwardly charming and cerebral, the Egyptian diplomat seemed to jump at every opportunity to keep Albright, and consequently, the United States, off balance. First elected to the post in 1990, Boutros-Ghali came to the job with an activist agenda and saw the US as a natural obstacle to his efforts to expand radically the UN's role in global diplomacy as well as that of the Secretary General's office.

As for his feelings about Albright, Boutros-Ghali may have harbored some resentment over the $1.1 billion in back dues owed by the US, or it may have been that, as a product of the third world, he felt somehow threatened by the might of the world's only remaining superpower and obliged to use his unique position to try to diminish the stature of the United States. Or it may have had to do with the fact that Albright was only one of seven female permanent representatives out of 185 in the General Assembly, as well as being the only woman to sit on the fifteen-member UN Security Council. And, while speculation about the reasons for the difficulty abounded, the end result was clear. Time and time again Boutros-Ghali would enlist the support of Albright and the US on matters of great importance, and time and time again, after weeks of negotiations to reach a unified position, the Secretary General would reverse his field, cutting some side deal with one of the US's countless antagonists in the General Assembly, or sometimes taking a completely new position altogether. Inevitably, this had the consequences of embarrassing Albright, and even more dangerous, undermining the national security interests of the United States.

Albright and many in the US Department of State had never supported his candidacy—the Bush administration had supported former Canadian Prime Minister Brian Mulroney and only accepted Boutros-Ghali as a compromise candidate—and held strong reservations that the Secretary General was able or even willing to achieve the far-reaching policy, administrative, and financial reforms that the US, Britain, and several other Western nations de-

manded. Ironically, the only two major reforms under-
taken during his tenure—adoption of a zero-growth
budget and appointment of an undersecretary for international oversight, the UN's version of an inspector general—had been rammed through the General Assembly
by the US Delegation. Albright herself felt caught in the
middle. As UN envoy she saw her job as not only representing the position and views of the United States before
the General Assembly, but also as providing the President
and Secretary of State Warren Christopher with a global
worldview from the outside, looking in at the United
States. In the view of those in the administration's foreign policy decision-making loop, especially Christopher,
this was an absolutely vital function. It was Albright's
fear, given the fact that Boutros-Ghali had effectively become a symbol of UN fiscal mismanagement to critics on
Capitol Hill, that there was no way Congress would appropriate payment of the delinquent dues payments so
long as this Secretary General remained in power. In effect, unless something was done, and soon, her credibility
among her peers in the General Assembly would be so
compromised that she would no longer be able to deliver
to the White House an honest, candid reflection of the
views of her fellow delegates.

On one front there was reason for optimism to believe
that the situation would resolve itself as Boutros-Ghali,
who accepted the position as Secretary General knowing
he was a compromise candidate, promised to serve only
one term, which was due to expire at the end of 1996.
Unfortunately, despite his commitment to leave, as the date

for his departure neared, Boutros-Ghali demonstrated no visible signs of going anywhere. It was Albright herself who alerted Christopher and the White House that the Secretary General's appointment calendar, his travel schedule, and overall agenda looked much more like that of a man campaigning for reelection rather than planning retirement. One senior State Department official described the prospect of enduring Boutros-Ghali for another term as an "unmitigated disaster."

Contrary to the many published accounts of the power struggle, notwithstanding Boutros-Ghali's willingness to appease anti-American factions within the UN, Albright's problems with the Secretary General were professional, not personal. In fact, during her first year as the US envoy, she and Boutros-Ghali still managed to dine privately once a month together. Albright has gone on record as saying that, at least initially, her problem was that the Secretary General often "overstepped his authority and believes he is in charge of everything." Nevertheless, as the months passed, incidents of Boutros-Ghali's disingenuousness and sandbagging of the United States became myriad. Obviously, the first and perhaps the most painful example was the 1993 Somalia disaster during which the Secretary General enlisted American support for a UN peacekeeping operation and publicly professed a commitment to a diplomatic solution, even though he was also actively pursuing an alternate agenda, which was tantamount to a military solution that would accept nothing less than the capture of Somali warlord General Farah Aidid. With good reason, many at the State Department still shudder at the thought of eighteen US Rangers being slaughtered during the ill-fated firefight at the Olympic Hotel in Mogadishu. The bitterness over the tragedy had only been exacerbated during the last few years by Boutros-Ghali's lack of remorse and unwillingness to accept his share of responsibility.

Another controversy that further ignited the passions of the opponents of the Egyptian diplomat, and continued to rankle the sensibilities of Albright and the Clinton administration was a heated exchange between the ambassador and Boutros-Ghali over whether the UN or NATO should maintain control over a peacekeeping force in the disputed region of Croatia known as Eastern Slavonia. The heated exchange occurred on December 15, 1995, within hours of the signing of the Paris Peace Treaty by all of the combatants in the bloody Bosnian conflict.

At a moment which should have been an hour of triumph for Albright, not to mention for Boutros-Ghali and the rest of the United Nations, the body was instead embroiled in an acrimonious dispute that by all accounts violated the decorum of the General Assembly in a manner not seen since Khrushchev beat his shoe on the podium thirty-five years earlier. The bone of contention, in essence, stemmed from a report by Boutros-Ghali recommending that the United Nations, following its lackluster peace-keeping efforts in Bosnia, resist assuming control of a new operation to be deployed to Eastern Slavonia. The region was captured by Serb forces in 1991, but as part of the peace agreement in the former Yugoslavia, the Serbs agreed to relinquish it to Croatian control under supervision of a multinational security force.

Boutros-Ghali, in the initial draft of his report, urged that the supervising force be a NATO unit, or at least one with some affiliation other than the United Nations. But, given that Eastern Slavonia was still technically part of occupied Serb territory, the United States did not want American forces under NATO control anywhere near the region. Unless the international community was willing to risk the perception that NATO forces had unilaterally invaded Serb territory, the Clinton administration felt strongly that the Slavonia mission should be under UN control. Well aware of the United States's position, Albright, after reviewing Boutros-Ghali's original report, encouraged him to modify it and instead present his preference as one of a menu of options, so as to avoid embarrassment, both to the UN and the United States, which did not enjoy being backed into a corner. Basically, the UN did not want the mission because Boutros-Ghali had finally concluded that it was beyond the capability of any force it could assemble. The Americans, on the other hand, did not want the mission because any way it played out, they lost. The moment US forces stepped foot in Slavonia, Serb leaders, in conjunction with extremist factions in the Russian republic, would denounce the American intrusion into the area, inevitably labeling it a violation of Serb sovereignty.

Unfortunately, the Secretary General's staff leaked the original report, undoubtedly betting that the US could not stand the heat. Predictably, Albright's response was swift and direct. She issued a statement that said simply, "I think it is misguided and counterproductive to argue that the UN should avoid this operation." Incredibly, this aroused the wrath of Boutros-Ghali like nothing else. Ultimately, the conflict escalated hours later to a contentious closed-door confrontation between the two diplomats. Boutros-Ghali, in a display of hypersensitivity rarely seen outside a men's singles final at Wimbledon, denounced Ambassador Albright's comments, expressing his "shock at the vulgarity of her statements." As for Albright, she had had enough already with the Secretary General's holier-than-thou attitude. "People's lives are hanging in the balance, for God's sake," she said to a colleague. Nevertheless, Albright exercised typical restraint, terming Boutros-Ghali's overreaction, and his characterizing of her words as "vulgar," "totally unacceptable." She added, quickly, in the interest of getting back to the important business of the General Assembly, that "she did not want to extend the disagreement with the Secretary General any further."

Notwithstanding the conciliatory attitude of Ambassador Albright, the timing of Boutros-Ghali's tantrum could not have been worse. The Peace Accords having been signed, the last obstacle for commitment of US troops to the region was about to be overcome. If Boutros-Ghali's actions were designed to steal President Clinton's thunder from the ceremony in Paris, it hardly worked. Rather, it was the latest in a long series of disputes that the US had had with the Secretary General over his belief that UN peacekeepers in the region lacked the authority and strength to be effective. More generally, American diplomats had complained often that they believe that Boutros-Ghali was more interested in promoting his own views and agenda than focusing on matters such as administration and consensus building.

At this point it is fair to ask, if Secretary General

Boutros Boutros-Ghali's term at the UN was such a disappointment, why was his ouster so pivotal a step in Madeleine Albright's career? At first glance, Boutros-Ghali's removal from office should have been an absolute nobrainer. On every level his performance was sub-par, and despite the fact that he did, in reality, have some noble intentions, most were never realized. Then, what was it that made his removal from office so difficult? What was it that made his ouster such a big deal? By way of explanation a recent comment by an African diplomat is telling. He observed that Madeleine Albright's efforts to oust Boutros Boutros-Ghali had the effect of "uniting the world . . . 184 nations against the United States." As it turned out, Secretary General Boutros-Ghali may have done a lousy job running the UN, but for the bulk of his fifty-year career he has been a model diplomat, serving in countless trouble spots, not the least of which included serving at the right hand of Egyptian President Anwar Sadat during the Camp David summit, which ultimately led to the historic Israeli-Egyptian Peace Accord. Despite his apparent distrust of the United States, he nevertheless commands unequivocal support from a number of world leaders such as French President Jacques Chirac and German Chancellor Helmut Kohl. Ironically, one of the Secretary General's unlikeliest supporters was former Bush administration Secretary of State Lawrence Eagleburger, who said, "The decision to dump Boutros-Ghali is dumb foreign policy and it doesn't move us anywhere at the UN. But I'm probably one of the few people who thinks he's done a good job." The fact is that Boutros-Ghali has always had considerable support within the General Assembly. In fact, the United States was the lone dissenter on the UN Security Council opposing the reappointment of the Secretary General, as all the other fourteen nations favored offering him a second term.

Moreover, even though Boutros-Ghali had pledged not to run, it is virtually unheard of at the United Nations to refuse any Secretary General a full turn, or more precisely, a second term in office. "Even Kurt Waldheim got a second term," points out a Boutros-Ghali supporter. For both Albright and the US, the stakes for removing the Secretary General from office were enormously high. Throughout the power struggle, Egyptian President Hosni Mubarak laid his reputation and prestige on the line as he supported Boutros-Ghali's bid for a second term. The administration risked complete alienation of the African, Asian, and Middle Eastern countries at the UN by potentially humiliating a man the third world considers one of their own. Had she been unsuccessful, the risk for Albright would have been even greater, inviting the inevitable blackball by her nemesis for the remainder of her tenure at the UN. What is more, by accepting the challenge that no one else in the administration was willing to undertake, she faced the very real possibility that failure in her mission could easily lead to a call for her resignation by some in the White House, and would certainly foreclose any possibility of her succeeding Warren Christopher at the State Department.

Nevertheless, Albright became convinced that she could never fulfill her mission as the US envoy as long as she was serving alongside a Secretary General who was by nature so antagonistic to American interests. With this in mind, the ambassador spearheaded the movement for change. Boutros-Ghali had to go. He had to go now.

In October 1995, at Albright's request, an interagency team was organized to draft a strategy paper that would lay out the justification for ousting Boutros-Ghali, as well as containing a short list of possible successors. The list was forwarded to Christopher and NSC Advisor Tony Lake by mid-January. Prominently positioned on the list was Boutros-Ghali's eventual successor, Kofi Annan, a Ghanian diplomat who had won the respect of many in the administration for his work monitoring the multitude of UN peacekeeping operations around the globe. For two months various drafts of the strategy were circulated among the interagency team as the officials carefully weighed the pros and cons of an effort to oust Boutros-Ghali, with the major downside being the very real possibility of failure, particularly if one of the perennial antagonists of the US, such as France, opted to use its Security Council veto to block the US.

On March 25, the final version of the paper was signed off on by President Clinton; it included a recommendation for a US endorsement of Annan. This was a matter in which Albright instructed all to proceed cautiously since the timing of publicly announcing American backing of a candidate was critical. The fact was, early in her term at the UN, Albright became aware that there was still enough anti-American sentiment in the General Assembly that a US endorsement of a nominee could quickly kill a potential candidate's chances for election. On Albright's recommendation, Washington officially denied backing Annan or any other candidate for several weeks. Ultimately, the plan involved informing Boutros-Ghali that the United States had made its decision and that its position was nonnegotiable. It went on to recommend that for the good of the international body, it was time for the longtime Egyptian emissary to consider a gracious, dignified exit from office, even retirement. It was also decided that Ambassador Albright—who as UN envoy, still had to conduct day-to-day business with the Secretary General—should formally disengage from the process.

Contrary to published reports, the United States, with Secretary of State Warren Christopher taking the lead, made a strong effort to cushion the blow to Boutros-Ghali, which included privately offering him a one-year extension until November of 1997. The logic was that the veteran diplomat could announce his retirement simultaneously with the celebration of his seventy-fifth birthday. By May of 1996 it appeared that a deal had been struck. However, a month later, and without explanation, the Secretary dug his heels in further, insisting on a two-and-one-half year extension. That was the final blow.

Deciding to play hardball, Christopher told *The New York Times* that, while it certainly was not his preferred means of solving a problem, the United States was ready to use its Security Council veto to deny Boutros-Ghali a second term if necessary.

Put simply, the result of this action was that all hell broke loose on the floor of the General Assembly. Ambassador Albright became the immediate target of vicious allegations that she was motivated by nothing more than personal contempt for the Secretary General, that she was conducting a vendetta against him. But even worse, the Clinton administration was in exactly the position that it dreaded; once again it was the United States versus the third world. As for the Western countries, their public position was that they had learned of the campaign to oust Boutros-Ghali in the press, while in fact, both Christopher and Albright had conducted extensive discussions with all of the major foreign capitals at each critical stage. Moreover, the Clinton White House produced phone records with leaders of Egypt, Russia, Germany, France, and Canada to back up their contention that they had not been acting completely alone. Unfortunately, this only served to throw gasoline on the fire as some nations, particularly France, accused the administration of making Boutros-Ghali's ouster a campaign issue. In reality, the Secretary General's tenure had, in fact, become a campaign issue, with Republican nominee Bob Dole grabbing every opportunity while on the campaign trail to decry America's role in the UN. Boutros-Ghali himself supported the view, saying, "I believe that the break came with the beginnings of attacks by Republicans—Dole's 'Booootros Boooootros-Ghali,' the black helicopters, and the bad image of the United Nations. The symbol of the United Nations is the Secretary General."

Ironically, the person who was the chief beneficiary of political capital from the administration's effort to oust Boutros-Ghali was not the President, but Madeleine Albright. While the White House categorically denied that its opposition to a second term for the Secretary General was motivated by a desire to neutralize attacks by the Dole campaign, no one could deny that Ambassador Albright's highly visible role in his ouster had made her the darling of the Republican right wing. This was particularly true of Senator Jesse Helms, who was so impressed by Albright, he remarked, "I've never in my life disagreed with someone so agreeable." Knowing that Helms's power and influence could not be underestimated, particularly in relation to the UN, Albright enthusiastically welcomed support from her newfound ally, frequently delivering foreign policy lectures at Helms's request to various groups in his home state. When asked what she was doing to promote a bipartisan foreign policy, Albright responded, "Honestly, there are only so many trips I can make to North Carolina."

This among other factors, such as President Clinton's steadily rising poll numbers in the area of foreign policy, served as fodder for those charging that the anti-Boutros-Ghali effort was just symptomatic of the Clinton White House cozying up to the conservatives in Congress. French President Jacques Chirac even went so far as to advise his fellow Security Council members that President Clinton was only playing politics, attempting to placate the right-wing segment of the American electorate, and after the presidential election in November, the United States would back down. He was wrong.

Not only would the United State refuse to back down, neither would Madeleine Albright, who found herself in a terribly awkward position. Tension between the US and the developing countries at the UN was running as high as it had in years. The Boutros-Ghali affair was getting very ugly and was beginning to cause collateral damage at the institution, eroding relationships between the US and some nations that had taken years to develop. Not only was Albright part of the problem, to some of her colleagues on the Security Council, she was the problem. Nevertheless, she was resolute. In her opinion, there was vital work that needed to be done around the world under the auspices of the United Nations. So long as Boutros-Ghali was in power the organization's focus would remain on petty, bureaucratic one-upmanship and posturing, not the difficult challenges that lay ahead. The choice was clear. Albright and the US had come too far to turn back.

After making one last try at accommodation, with Albright suggesting to Boutros-Ghali that he assume the ceremonial post of Secretary General Emeritus, the Clinton administration took two decisive steps to demonstrate US resolve. First, on November 19, a full two weeks after the President's election victory, Ambassador Albright did what Warren Christopher had promised, casting the lone veto against a second term for the embattled Secretary General. Of course, the French retaliated in typical fashion, threatening that it would use its veto to block any US nominee who was not fluent in French. Albright took the position that for the moment the US did not have a nominee. It was also rumored that the French ambassador's threat gave her a tremendous laugh. "Are they aware that almost every delegate in the General Assembly speaks French?" she is said to have asked incredulously.

If using the veto got the attention of the General Assembly, then the second step knocked it out. President Clinton, in naming Madeleine Albright as his next Secretary of State, not only made history, but also vindicated her tough words and deeds during the previous four years at the United Nations. Suddenly, her detractors and enemies in the General Assembly—an inevitable by-product of controversies such as Somalia, Bosnia, and Rwanda—were sent a signal. And that included supporters of Boutros Boutros-Ghali. "Everyone saw her as someone to fear, to be in awe of. Everyone wanted to be able to present themselves as her special friend and not get on her bad side," said a UN colleague.

On December 13, 1996, Kofi Annan was unanimously elected as the UN Secretary General. Madeleine Albright had taken on a fight no one in the administration wanted, but which everyone agreed had to be won. She easily could have lost everything: her job, her prestige, her career. Yet knowing this, Albright pressed forward in the belief that if the United Nation's charter is ever to be fulfilled, effective leadership by its Secretary General is absolutely imperative. The power struggle with Boutros-Ghali could easily have turned into Albright's diplomatic Waterloo, but instead she was credited with masterminding a strategy that installed a leader who was decidedly pro-reform and vastly more pro-American than his predecessor. Beyond that, her efforts, in the opinion of many, left the institution of the United Nations stronger, more effective, and ultimately more cohesive than it had been in decades.

9

A FAMILY AFFAIR

Discovery of a

Newfound Heritage and the

Meaning of Friendship

It should have been one of the happiest days of her life. It should have been exciting. It should have been fun. Unfortunately, for Madeleine Albright, her first day on the job at Foggy Bottom was anything but fun.

Not twenty-four hours had passed since the Senate had voted unanimously to confirm her nomination as this country's first female Secretary of State when the very public love affair between Albright and the media abruptly came to a halt. Since she had arrived at the office only minutes before, her first cup of coffee was still piping hot when the intercom buzzed.

"Your daughter Anne is on the line," began her assistant. "She says it's urgent."

Albright's heart skipped a beat. For her entire career, wherever she was, no matter what her position, she had a standing rule: If her children called the office, they were to be put right through, no questions asked. The reason didn't matter. If it was important to one of her kids, it was important to her. It did not make sense that her daughter would feel it necessary to explain the urgency of the call. Something was wrong. Albright quickly picked up the phone. As she did so, the grandmother of two had an awful thought. "Are the babies all right?"

After reassuring her mother that the grandchildren were fine, Anne informed Albright that she had just received a phone call at her law office from Michael Dobbs, a *Washington Post* reporter. Dobbs, it turned out, was about to break a story that stated that the Secretary's grandparents were not Catholics, as she had always believed, but were in fact Jewish and that they along with at least a dozen of her relatives had died in the Holocaust. In one respect, Albright was relieved, although in another, still somewhat taken aback by the revelation. For several more minutes mother and daughter spoke as Albright made sure she understood every detail of Dobbs's story. By the end of the day Dobbs was in the Secretary's office presenting his evidence.

To Albright, Dobbs's revelation about her family's Jewish heritage was not all that surprising. In fact, it was Albright herself who brought this to the attention of Clinton confidant Vernon Jordan, who was overseeing the vetting of all key appointments at the State Department. She explained that "With the opening up of the Czech Republic, I as UN ambassador began to get some mail—frankly, a lot of mail—about helping people in the Czech Republic and bringing them here or providing health care for them. I got some letters about my family; some that was off by thirty or forty years; some that indicated some of my family, or my family, was of Jewish origin." Once her own suspicions were aroused, she began to delve into her past. According to senior advisor James Rubin, while on a ski vacation in Aspen over the Christmas holiday, Albright had polled her siblings on the subject. "She asked her brother and sister if their grandmother had ever told them any stories. They all asked the obvious questions, but nobody knew anything."

After she was formally nominated as Secretary of State, the letters from the Czech Republic began to flood in. "On the basis of that and some additional information, I concluded—it was clear that my family was of Jewish origin," explained Albright to *ABC News*. But other than alerting the State Department, the Secretary-designate let the matter rest until *The Washington Post* ran Dobbs's story. Almost immediately she called the White House, communicating the news of her new genealogical background directly to President Clinton, who found it "fascinating," and encouraged Albright to explore her background further. And, as White House spokesman Mike McCurry noted, the President was adamant that the revelation would have no effect on Albright's status as the nation's top diplomat. "Americans of Christian, Jewish, and Muslim faiths are participating in the search for peace in the Mideast, and Albright's roots should not affect her position as a key US player in the peace process," stated McCurry on behalf of the administration. President Clinton's strong empathy with Albright's predicament is understandable in light of two factors. One, her ancestry really was irrelevant to her qualifications for and ultimate selection as Secretary of State. And two, the President himself, during his first term in office, was made aware that he had a long-lost half-brother about whom his family never spoke. Not unlike Albright, the President had received this revelation after living more than four decades without so much as a hint about it.

For Albright a far greater shock than the discovery concerning her heritage was the new knowledge that three of her grandparents had perished at the hands of the Nazis. Although she professes no direct recollection of them— Albright was two years old the last time she saw them— the inhuman and violent nature of their fate was no less unsettling. According to the Secretary, while she had some hint about her own ancestry, the true facts surrounding her grandparents' demise caught her completely off guard. "At some point I learned that my grandparents had died during the war. That seemed a perfectly logical answer. If you're eight years old and you are told that your grandparents died, and you think of grandparents as being old people, then you don't question it." But the truth, which was denied to Albright for fifty years, was that her grandparents did not just die in the war.

Albright's paternal grandparents were named Arnost

and Olga Korbel. They were longtime natives of Prague, who like the 90,000 other Czech Jews were required, after the German occupation in 1939, to register property, wear gold stars signifying their Jewishness on their clothing, and abide by severe restrictions on their ability to travel. Still, for a time, their treatment was mild compared to what was happening elsewhere in Europe. But by 1941 all that had changed as the Nazi occupation force decreed that all Jews in or around Prague would be relocated to the garrison town of Terezín, which was really nothing more than an ancient, fortresslike prison, with barracks that could accommodate roughly 5,000 inmates, nowhere near the 50,000 Jews who would eventually be sent there. Although completely unsuited to house such a large inmate population, it ultimately served as a huge holding area, a way station for the thousands of Czech Jews destined for Auschwitz. Arnost and Olga Korbel arrived in Terezín in the summer of 1942 on a freight train along with more than nine hundred others from Prague. By September, Arnost died from undetermined causes, although malnutrition, gastroenteritis, and typhoid were rampant throughout the camp. As winter engulfed the region, Albright's maternal grandmother, Anna Spieglova, arrived along with several other relatives. While it appeared from murky records that Spieglova died at Terezín, Olga Korbel apparently survived incarceration until 1944 and was on one of the last transport trains designated for Auschwitz. Of the 1,714 people aboard the freight train, all but 250 were sent directly to the gas chambers. The rest, in apparent good health, were sent to the labor camps. After almost four years of enduring the cruelties of Terezín, Olga Korbel was not among them.

To make matters worse, while the Secretary was still reeling from the horrific details of her grandparents' demise, sources in the Israeli government leaked word that its intelligence service, the Mossad, had first uncovered evidence of Albright's Jewish ancestry in 1995 and had been closely monitoring the situation for years. This was the last thing Albright needed, as a wide range of skeptics throughout the world were rapidly beginning to question her veracity on the subject of her lineage. Some suggested that although she had to have known more than she was letting on, it was still a personal matter. Others, however, went so far as to accuse her of lying outright in a vain attempt to conceal her Jewish background. The fact was that both theories were wrong, and whatever story the Israelis were circulating was a mystery to Albright, who had never knowingly had a conversation with any member of the Israeli intelligence service. As it stood, the newly appointed Secretary of State was tremendously relieved that her boss had been so sympathetic over the issue and had refused to pass judgment on her.

Nevertheless, despite the tremendous turmoil and distraction caused by the media attention to the story, Albright refused to walk on eggshells and let the story blow over, as some of her State Department colleagues had advised. She had been a player in Washington long enough to know that there are two kinds of news stories, ones that have "legs" and others that don't. The term refers to whether or not a story contains enough controversy and truth to stay on the front page day after day, long enough, that is, to get picked up by news services and affiliates nationwide. Albright was savvy enough to realize that despite the fact that the media fascination with her background was really much ado about nothing, the story was snowballing fast enough that it would soon become much more than a typical inside-the-Beltway melodrama. One nervous White House flack remarked, "Does this story have legs? You're damned right it does. This story has legs that would make an NFL running back green with envy!" It was clear to the Secretary that this story was not going to blow over any time soon, particularly if she danced around the issue. So with this in mind, coupled with the strong belief that she had nothing to hide, Albright decided to pull no punches and met her critics head-on.

Very publicly, the Secretary of State responded to those that doubted her candor about having been surprised by the discovery of her Jewish heritage. "That's their problem. I know what I know, and my parents—there were no holes in their story. I wish I'd known earlier, and I just feel that people should look into their own lives. I'm never going to satisfy everybody on this score. I'm sorry about that, but I know what I know, and I know when I knew it." In attempting to put this in context, Albright talked openly of a time her brother, John, visited their father's hometown in the early nineties in an attempt to dig into their family tree. "He asked a lot of questions. Nobody said one word to him and his name is John Korbel, not that different from Josef," she explained, referring to her late father.

In major interviews with *Newsweek* and several other

publications, Albright made no secret of how she felt about her parents' actions. "I'm very proud of what my parents did for me and my brother and my sister. I was very close to them. I am not going to question their motives. In terms of my basic beliefs, I have not had to change anything. I have always been very proud of my heritage. And as I find out more about it, I am even more proud."

Ironically, the really enticing story surrounding the unearthing of Albright's genealogical baggage lay not in the disclosure of new and interesting information concerning the Secretary's background, but rather in the completely unprecedented media onslaught that ensued so soon after her confirmation. Within a week of Michael Dobbs's story hitting the streets, no fewer than seventy-five major publications picked up the story. In addition to every major television network, radio syndicates and large independent stations in major markets all assigned top reporters to monitor the progress of the story. And that was just in the continental United States. Given Secretary Albright's global reputation as world citizen, the thirst for even the most insignificant information concerning her background went well beyond American borders. As one reporter from a British tabloid said, "Everyone loves an icon, but not as much as an icon with a skeleton in her closet."

While this may have been the mentality of some in the media who worked the story, it was off base. As any friend or colleague of Albright's will attest, notwithstanding her heartache at learning the fate of her grandparents, the disclosure of her Jewish lineage was no big deal. Former vice presidential candidate Geraldine Ferarro put it this way,

"If you know Madeleine, who was raised in many different places around many different cultures, the disclosure is kind of irrelevant. She has always detested any kind of racism, whatever form it takes. To her, anti-Semitism is another form of racism, and she condemned it long before the disclosure and she will condemn it long after. To her it was kind of like, 'Okay, this doesn't change anything. Now let's get back to work.' "

And somehow, some way, Madeleine Albright managed to do just that. By rejecting every recommendation from her media advisors and hitting the airwaves to tell her side of the story, she prevailed over the proprietors of innuendo and gossip. Perhaps most startling was the unusual method of spin control used by the Secretary, which effectively was no spin control whatsoever. Her plan was simple. Albright knew that she had nothing to hide, that there were no skeletons lurking in her closet, that if the American people only heard the truth from her own mouth, then they would believe her. Many in the administration were skeptical and advised against pursuing such a course of action. One person who was not skeptical was President Clinton, who knew that Madeleine Albright's greatest asset was simply being Madeleine Albright. With the President's blessing the new Secretary of State took her show on the road, appearing on virtually all the Sunday morning news shows over an eight-day period. By the time she completed her media blitz, which was facetiously referred to by White House dissenters as "letting Madeleine be Madeleine," she had almost single-handedly quelled the firestorm. The daily updates on her background stopped appearing, then dropped back to once a week. And shortly after her first trip abroad the story basically disappeared from the headlines.

Albright's defiance of convention, by putting up her own personal credibility head-to-head with that of the media, was typical of her business-as-usual approach to solving problems. No matter what the challenge, regardless of the personal sacrifice, the job has to get done. And while this go-for-it attitude has been an inexorable part of her enormously charismatic public persona, it would be unfair not to make note of the fact that Madeleine Albright is still only human and suffered a considerable amount of pain as a result of the media circus that surrounded the disclosure. Shortly after the story broke, she spoke with longtime friend, journalist Kati Marton, who herself discovered her Jewish ancestry as a middle-aged adult. As Marton tells it, "I felt great sympathy for the emotional upheaval she was experiencing. 'Tell me,' she said, 'how did you deal with this? What did you tell your children?' "

In one respect, Madeleine Albright was herself a direct victim of the Holocaust, a victim whose parents were so horrified by their experiences that they became convinced that being Jewish was tantamount to a death sentence. A condition so potentially fatal that they felt compelled to deny her knowledge of the Korbel family's ethnic background. That it was courageous on their part, an act of true love for their children is beyond question, but that such a decision carried long-term consequences is undeniable. To hear others who have gone through similar unexpected, midlife ancestral revelations speak on the subject, the effect on their personal lives is often one of ongoing reassessment of their cultural identities. But, according to Walter Reich, director of the US Holocaust Museum, "What makes Albright's experience different is not its poignancy, but its extreme publicity. She must rework her sense of identity at the same time that she must contend with a challenging and sometimes intrusive press." Odds are that the discovery concerning her family's background will have minimal impact on Albright the diplomat. On a personal level, however, only time will tell what effect the disclosure will have. But one thing is for sure, if Madeleine Albright needs a shoulder to cry on, there are literally hundreds of available shoulders in New York and Washington waiting in the wings.

Senator Barbara Mikulski could not have been more clear. Over and over again, the four-foot-eleven fireball from Maryland made the point, at least four or five different ways. "The reason Madeleine Albright has so many loyal friends in this town is because she truly understands the meaning of being a friend." At the moment, Mikulski was not speaking of the time when she had been brutally mugged and beaten right outside her rowhouse in downtown Baltimore and the first person who came calling was Madeleine Albright. This, despite the fact that the UN ambassador had spent most of the day participating in an arduous round of negotiations in a closed Security Council session and had to travel three hours just to look in on the diminutive senator. Rather, Mikulski was referring to the countless instances when she would call Albright for advice, professional and personal, or sometimes just to vent after a tough day. For Mikulski, her friendship with Madeleine Albright represents a rare blend of mutual respect and simple, relaxed comradeship.

For a person as dynamic, and just plain busy as she often is, Secretary Albright is uniquely available to her friends and family. Syndicated columnist Mary McGrory, who counts herself as one of the legion of FOMs—Friends of Madeleine—that populate Washington, has commented that Albright possesses a "strong strain of maternal solicitude and is universally known around town as a good soul." Indeed, in one of the most cutthroat settings imaginable, Albright has built unusually strong bridges with her friends and colleagues, bridges built on a loyalty and affection so strong that it seems out of place in a town like Washington, more like something one might see in a small town in the Midwest. But to hear her close friends tell it, to Albright the location or setting tends to be irrelevant. Friendship is friendship, period.

Several people tell the story of the time early in her term as UN ambassador when the husband of Congresswoman Barbara Kennelly suffered a fatal stroke. Kennelly and Albright had been close friends for over a decade, and Albright was deeply saddened by her friend's tragic loss. On the day of the funeral few expected to see Albright, given the impossible nature of her schedule and the fact that the service was being held in Connecticut, three hours from Manhattan. But it never occurred to Albright not to attend.

In fact, sources at the UN have said that the second the date of the service was announced, she ordered her scheduler to clear her calendar. And while mutual friends speak glowingly of the considerable time and trouble to which Albright went in order to be with her friend on that sad day, Albright scoffs at such comments. It was not a matter of trouble or inconvenience, but rather a matter of respect. Quite simply, it was the right thing to do.

Geraldine Ferraro offers a similar experience, telling of a time during the mid-1980s when Albright was spending the weekend at one of the Ferraro family's vacation homes on Fire Island, outside New York City. This weekend escape haven, which is reachable only by boat, was particularly crowded with city dwellers that steamy July weekend, making getting on or off the island problematic at best. After a long day of sun and sailing the Ferraro family, along with "Aunt" Madeleine, cooked up a feast to rival the best seafood haunts between Nagshead and Nantucket. Late into the night, as a storm front moved in, Ferraro, her husband, John Zaccaro, and Albright reminisced about old times, like the time the two women shared an all-night train ride together from Moscow to Leningrad during which they were fortified by a ration of vodka and Fritos. Between claps of thunder they shared war stories about the Carter years, the 1984 convention, and New York politics. Predictably, countless tales of parenthood crept into the conversation. As Ferraro put it, except for the weather, "The weekend could not have been more perfect had it been scripted."

And then it happened. Just past midnight a phone call

came from the cardiac unit at St. John's Hospital in Queens informing Ferraro that her elderly mother had been rushed to the hospital by ambulance after being stricken with a major heart attack.

Bad weather was rapidly engulfing the island, and Ferraro knew that the last ferry would be leaving for the mainland within the hour. Quickly Ferraro packed a bag while her husband went to awaken their son. As Ferraro tried to apologize to Albright for their unexpected departure, her friend cut her off. "Gerri, let the boy sleep. There's no reason for everyone to go out in this weather. I'll go with you—"

"But Madeleine . . . ," protested Ferraro.

"Don't be ridiculous," said Albright, refusing to take no for an answer. "It's settled. I'm going."

So, in the middle of the night, a onetime vice presidential nominee and a future Secretary of State put on rain slickers and made their way through a torrential downpour to the dock, where they boarded the last ferry to Long Island. The summer squall had had the effect of turning a twenty-minute boat ride into an hour of choppy seas and forty-mph-plus force winds. Eventually they made it to shore, taking Ferraro's car to the hospital. Upon their arrival the two women experienced something completely unfamiliar in their professional experience: total powerlessness. The fate of Ferraro's mother was in the hands of a faceless team of cardiologists who had neither the time nor the inclination to deal with loved ones. In other words, Ferraro and Albright were helpless to do anything. Anything, that is, but wait and pray. So, with few other options available, they spent the night in the lobby of St. John's intensive care ward, waiting, hoping for the best. Together, they went to the hospital chapel to pray. Every couple of hours one of the doctors would appear, telling them that the cardiac team was doing all that they could, but that it was too soon to tell. This pattern continued throughout the night as the hours passed. Finally, by morning, as the sun rose over the East River, word came from the doctors that Ferraro's mother had turned the corner, that her condition was stable.

On a lighter note, Ferraro loves to tell of the time, right in the middle of Albright's confirmation hearings, that her family received an extraordinary gift from the Secretary-designate. As it happened, during the same week, Ferraro's daughter-in-law, Natalie Zaccaro, had given birth to the family's first grandchild, a little girl. As might be expected, an excited Ferraro called several close friends with the wonderful news. And while Albright was at the top of her call list, Ferraro was certain that reaching her during confirmation week would be nearly impossible. So, after a couple of tries, she just left a message, knowing that Albright would call back as soon as humanly possible.

For the next few days Ferraro went about the business of being a new grandmother, helping the young family get settled. Every few hours she would turn on CNN or call mutual friend Barbara Mikulski in Washington to see how things were going with Albright's confirmation, knowing that it could be days before the two were likely to talk directly. Toward the end of the week a knock came at the door. It was a courier with a special-delivery package.

Ferraro signed for the package and handed it to Natalie. Upon opening the package they were amazed by its contents. Inside was a baby gift from Albright, a tiny Baby Madeleine Doll, with a note that read as follows: "To Natalie. I've always wanted a little girl to give this to, and now I finally do." What amazed Ferraro was not the sweetness or the thoughtfulness of the gift. To know her friend was to expect such gestures. Rather, what was incredible was how Albright—with all that she was going through, all the briefings, all the interviews, all the studying—could have found the time to buy the gift, write the note, and have the gift delivered to Natalie's front door. "Vintage Madeleine," says Ferraro.

Fortunately, not all of Albright's good deeds are confined to life and death situations. Take the time in 1988 when a Czech-American philanthropist, Josiah Auspitz, called Albright seeking advice on how to best channel humanitarian and medical aid to Czechoslovakia. According to Auspitz, it went something like this: "I called her cold. I introduced myself as an officer of a charitable organization that had been donating books in Poland and Hungary. Up to this point, Czechoslovakia had not even allowed its physicians to receive substantial donations of professional literature from the West." Auspitz went on to tell Albright that, in response to an outcry among the Czech medical community, the Prague government relented and decided to authorize the acceptance of twenty thousand advanced medical textbooks to shore up the pitiful resources of the Czech Ministry of Health. The problem, explained Auspitz, was that the publishing houses wanted to make delivery of the books before the end of the tax year. The issue was how to pay for the shipping cost. "Do you have any suggestions?" he asked.

"Well, you know, I could do this."

Auspitz was taken aback. He was seeking her insights into the complexities of the Czech bureaucracy. He had not called her seeking money, and told her so.

"I know, but I could do this," said Albright. "Would you like a check?"

For a man who spent virtually every day trying to convince people of the worthiness of his cause, a conversation with Madeleine Albright was a welcome respite. Not only was she willing to listen, but she was absolutely insistent on helping out. After Auspitz explained that what was really needed was a financial guarantee in case of a mishap in the shipment, Albright didn't miss a beat. "Well, you've got it. Send me a bill for what you can't raise."

In the end, the books found their way to Prague. But Albright's commitment to the cause wasn't finished. In 1990, after the Velvet Revolution had restored democracy to Czechoslovakia, Albright delivered a contribution that subsidized a full-scale book donation program to her former homeland. At first, Albright the philanthropist requested anonymity. But later, after being named ambassador to the United Nations, she permitted disclosure of her identity, reasoning that it might have the effect of encouraging others to support the initiative. As for the end result, it is best explained by a direct beneficiary of the program, Czech biologist Pavol Demes, who provides the following perspective. "It may be hard to comprehend how much the gift of books meant for my country. The first shipment of books . . . was welcomed with a brass band. . . . And then with reports on national television." As a result of the program, more than 300,000 English-language books, journals, and CD-ROMs from the US have arrived in Prague. To many in the newly free Czech Republic, "It continues to be one of the most visible, direct, and personal forms of Western assistance."

In attempting to uncover the source of Albright's humanitarianism, a conviction that runs particularly deep when it comes to the Czech Republic, one need look no farther than her family tree. By her own admission, much of what Albright believes in, has striven for, and has accomplished throughout her life has been a direct result of the influence of her father, Josef Korbel. "My own world-view consists largely of ideas my father implanted on me," she has said. "He was a great intellectual humanist." Albright's brother, John Korbel, bears witness to this, saying, "Madeleine had a special relationship with our father. In part because she followed so closely in his footsteps." But, even though Albright's father was her intellectual mentor, this was only one aspect of a deep and loyal commitment between parent and child. To hear the Korbel siblings tell it, the essence of the relationship between Josef Korbel and his children stemmed from just plain old love and affection. "The most severe form of punishment was when our father wouldn't talk to us for a week," explains John. Albright herself recalls only two major arguments she ever had with her father. Both came when Albright was a teenager. The first came just before her freshman year, when her father insisted that his daughter enroll in a prestigious private school that had offered her a scholarship. Young Madeleine, wanting so badly to be the consummate American teen, wanted to attend the local public high school. Eventually she relented, admitting now that "the school did give me a tremendous education." The other argument concerned the senior prom when Albright's father refused to permit Madeleine to ride in her date's car. The diplomatic solution? The sixteen-year-old Albright was allowed to ride to the prom with her date, but with Mr. Korbel following close behind in his own vehicle. Ultimately, father and daughter put these minor disputes behind them and remained, in the words of her siblings, "the best of friends."

It is important to understand that, in Madeleine Albright's world, friendship is a two-way street. While there are any number of FOMs ready and willing to recount Albright's seemingly endless good deeds, the FOMs are also an extremely protective bunch that throws pretense out the window when it comes to protecting Albright. One prominent example of this occurred in the early 1980s, when Carter lost, the Republicans regained control of the Senate, and her husband, journalist Joe Albright, suddenly announced that "our marriage is over and I'm in love with someone else." By Albright's own admission, she did not see the breakup coming. "It was a shock. I had been married twenty-three years and I did not want a divorce." "It made her reevaluate her life," says her friend Winifred Freund. "But it contributed to her strength." For a number of years, by many accounts, Albright remained bitter. But, rather than encourage her on a downward spiral, several close friends approached her, telling her in no uncertain terms that it was time to shut up about her ex and get on with her life. Apparently it worked.

Throughout such trials as her divorce and the revelation concerning her family history, Albright has had one network of support that, above all others, has been more dear to her than anything, her three daughters, Katie, Alice, and Anne. Throughout her career, work and family had clearly defined boundaries, and there was never any question which came first. As Anne, who describes herself as "one of the three leading experts on her mother," put it, "As kids, we never felt we were being sacrificed for her career."

As adults, the bond between Albright and her children appears solid as ever but not because of her newly attained stature. Rather, it seems to have evolved from a steady, long-term pattern of positive reinforcement dating from when her daughters were quite young. "When we were children, my younger sister, Katie, wanted to be a fireman. My twin sister, Alice, wanted to be a doctor. I wanted to be a baseball player, a pitcher for the New York Mets. My mom never told us, you should do this or you should do that," says Anne. To Albright, parenting was about encouraging her children to do their best to be the best. And, according to her children, throughout their lives she was right there helping them as they pursued their dreams. But as Anne is careful to point out, her mother is a strong believer that "there's no such thing as luck. What you get you work for."

In taking stock of Madeleine Albright's incredible life,

one can safely say that by serving as the US ambassador to the United Nations and as a member of the National Security Council, and by reaching the pinnacle achievement of being named Secretary of State, she has gotten exactly what she has worked for. But stay tuned.

Madeleine Albright never stops working.

10

EPILOGUE

It was standing room only at the exclusive Halcyon House ballroom in downtown Washington. Over two hundred of Madeleine Albright's closest friends had assembled on this warm Saturday night for a celebration. The guest list included the President and the First Lady, Senators Leahy, Mikulski, and Helms, and Czech President Václav Havel, who had flown in from Prague especially for the occasion. Best buddy Geraldine Ferraro was one of six guests asked to give a toast. Another was senior aide James Rubin, who had them rolling in the aisles with jokes about Secretary Albright's budding career as an author, announcing, tongue in cheek, that his boss was working on such projects as *Saddami Dearest, Deck the Halls with Boutros-Ghali,* and the essential *Diplomat's Guide to Spanish Slang.*

Most in attendance were there to celebrate the sixtieth birthday of one of the most colorful and extraordinary lives of the twentieth century. But for the first woman to hold the office of Secretary of State, May 15, 1997, was an occasion of many anniversaries. It was almost thirty-eight years to the day that twenty-two-year-old Madeleine had graduated from Wellesley College, where she earned her B.A. in political science. What's more, given that Albright was wed within days of her commencement, this same weekend would have also marked almost four decades of matrimony had her marriage held together. Indeed, the fifteenth also bore a modicum of professional significance, as it was exactly three months earlier that Secretary Albright stepped aboard a specially chartered US Air Force jet and embarked on her first diplomatic mission in her unprecedented role. But for all the symbolism and coincidence that filled the night, there was one milestone that stood out for Albright and her brain trust. While most of the crowd came to wish Madeleine Albright a happy sixtieth birthday, those in her inner circle couldn't help raising a glass and drinking a toast to the passage of Secretary of State Madeleine Albright's very successful first hundred days in office.

Since being confirmed on January 23, 1997, Secretary Albright had pursued an ambitious agenda that combined substance and symbolism in defining her role as the top

United States diplomat. In Albright's view, in the post–Cold War world the American people have become disconnected from their nation's mission abroad. As she saw it, her challenge was to convince this country's citizens that they "have a stake in America's foreign policy." Toward this end, Secretary Albright set the bar high, promising early on to strive to restore "a compact between Congress and the American people" on the subject. The goal as set forth was as lofty as it was enlightened. The why of it was obvious, but the how part still required some doing. After all, admits Albright, "Foreign policy is a hard sell in a post-Soviet age when the public wants the benefits of peace, not the burdens of global responsibility."

As it turned out, an apathetic body politic wasn't Albright's only problem. Just hours after assuming the helm at Foggy Bottom she found herself in the awkward position of having to recapture many of the powers and responsibilities delegated to her by Warren Christopher when she served as UN ambassador in the administration's first term. Clearly, while Albright had enjoyed the vast level of authority afforded her as the most powerful envoy in history, much of her autonomy was a function of the global imperatives of the era, in countries such as Haiti, Bosnia, and Rwanda. But with most of these trouble spots stabilized, experts agreed that it only made sense for the foreign policy decision-making apparatus of the US to revert to the centralized control of the State Department. The irony of this was not lost on Albright. Only in Washington could a cabinet official end up in a power struggle with oneself.

Notwithstanding the obstacles that lay ahead, Secretary

of State Albright set the wheels in motion from the very first moment of her swearing-in. Her first directive was to order that the portrait of former Secretary of State George Marshall, the architect of the Marshall Plan, be hung in a prominent place in her office. At lunch, she dined with the rank-and-file staff in the State Department cafeteria. By the end of the day, Albright had ordered her top assistants to plan and book a nine-nation, eleven-day trip so that she could meet officially with the heads of state of several of this country's major allies and trading partners.

The first stop on the European leg of Secretary Albright's tour was Italy, a choice that was questioned by many, given that incoming Secretaries of State have traditionally made their inaugural visits to such long-standing allies as Britain or France. However, Albright's selection, while seemingly unorthodox, was clearly by design. There, she used the occasion to drum up support for an expanded NATO, fully aware that the Rome government, headed by Prime Minister Romano Prodi strongly favored such a restructuring, especially to the east. Knowing that she would be sitting down with President Yeltsin in Moscow within the week, Albright used her captive audience to implore Russian leaders to abandon Cold War "old think" and establish a means for an ongoing dialogue with the West on NATO. She also didn't mince words on Italy's business and trade dealings with Libya and Iraq, warning that the US was greatly disturbed by the Prodi government's relations with rogue states. By the time Albright bid her hosts *arrivederci*, the Italian press had dubbed her the Iron Lady of American foreign policy, with one journalist calling her the "second coming of Margaret Thatcher."

From Rome it was on to Brussels, the home of NATO, where Albright wasted no time lining up the support of fifteen allied foreign ministers for a bigger, more inclusive strategic partnership. Best of all, she secured the commitment of the ministers to agree by July 7—the date of the next NATO summit in Madrid—on a timetable to determine in which order the European nations will become full members of NATO.

By the time Secretary Albright arrived in Moscow, stepping off the Air Force jet wearing a cozy Hudson Bay coat and a Stetson cowboy hat, Yeltsin, Foreign Minister Yevgeny Primakov, and the rest of the Russian cabinet had no way of knowing what to expect from Albright, only that she would not show up empty-handed. Their instincts proved correct, as the top American envoy carried with her a portfolio that included a NATO-Russian consultation schedule, a new treaty cutting conventional arms in Europe, and a plan for a joint NATO-Russian peacekeeping brigade. And while Yeltsin and his advisors were lukewarm to many of Albright's proposals, in recognition of her solid base of support among the European foreign ministers, they made the decision to remain at the negotiating table. Unbeknownst to the Russians, that was all that Albright wanted in the short run, as her true goal was to establish a framework for substantive negotiations that would continue at the March 21 Helsinki summit between President Clinton and Boris Yeltsin. As it turned out, significant progress was made at the summit in the areas of START II and III, the ABM treaty, and the Chemical Weapons Agreement. According to Albright, at Helsinki, "We were able to talk about a NATO-Russia charter, which would allow

Russia to feel that it was at the table in a series of discussions about the future of Europe, not to have a veto, but a voice."

Two other key stops for Albright were Seoul and Beijing. First, on the way to Seoul, the Secretary visited Camp Bonifas, the last outpost of the Cold War. Taking a helicopter ride in the demilitarized zone between South Korea and the Communist North—an area that many observers view as the most volatile flashpoint in the world—Albright was able to get a firsthand view of the armed encampment called North Korea. On the ground she had the opportunity to meet and greet some of the 37,000 US troops still stationed there. During one address to a packed auditorium of American GIs, she wowed the crowd when she announced, "I don't know what it is, but I just have this thing for men in uniform." Upon her arrival in Seoul, representatives from both the South and the North announced that they had agreed to enter into discussions as a precursor to peace talks. The conference, as it was referred to, was held in New York on March 5, 1997. US officials linked North Korean participation to the fact that its economy is very nearly bankrupt and that many of its twenty million people are near starvation.

As for the final stop on Albright's first trip abroad, fate seemed to save the most complicated encounter for last. Since the day of her nomination, Albright could not make a public appearance without someone in the media asking her to clarify her position on the People's Republic of China. Where did she stand on Most Favored Nation trading status? What about Hong Kong? But more than anything, the press wanted to know where exactly the Secretary of State stood in regard to Beijing's horrendous human rights record. To each question, Albright sought to remain steadfast in her response. While the US–Chinese relationship was far from perfect, "relations between the two countries cannot be held hostage to any one issue." She is also quick to point out that China is "a country with whom we have many business dealings—in trying to control nuclear proliferation. They signed the Nuclear Non-Proliferation Treaty, the Comprehensive Test Ban Treaty. They are working with us in trying to resolve how to deal with North Korea and Cambodia. So it's a complex relationship."

If Secretary Albright considered US–Chinese relations to be complex before her trip last February, things suddenly got much more complicated only days before her scheduled arrival, when the longtime political leader of the People's Republic, Party Chairman, Deng Xiaoping, unexpectedly died. Suffice it to say, with the entire Chinese government in disarray, this would have been ample reason for Beijing to tell the State Department to postpone Albright's visit. Somewhat surprisingly, particularly in light of the controversy surrounding Albright's not forgotten participation in the UN Conference on Women there in 1995, the Beijing government encouraged her not to cancel her plans.

Arriving the night before Deng's funeral, the Secretary of State conducted a full round of talks focusing on nuclear proliferation, North Korea, and the future of Hong Kong. Upon her return, Albright was pleased to report transitional leaders expressed a strong willingness to maintain a level of continuity in the onetime British protectorate, recognizing the severe political and financial consequences of a botched transition of power.

And while the new Secretary of State returned home to kudos and accolades resulting from her first trip abroad, she confided to her colleagues that she was pleased to get it out of the way, so that she could get down to business and pursue her chief objective of "creating foreign policy machinery that reflects post-Cold War realities, that is suitable to the way we see our goals and our interests." Mindful of the fact that less than one percent of the entire federal budget is spent on foreign relations, Albright spent much of her first hundred days in office trying, in her words, "to recapture resources that are necessary for carrying out our foreign policy." How she went about this was nothing short of remarkable. During a span of less than three months Albright made four times as many trips inside US borders than outside. A typical week included appearances or delivering speeches in Colorado, Texas, Michigan, and North Carolina—a frequent stop for the Secretary, due in large part to her close relationship with Jesse Helms. Two months into her term, she implemented the practice of floating all of her speeches on the Internet on the State Department Home Page, under the menu heading, "Reaching Out To Americans."

In addition to her successes abroad, Secretary Albright's efforts during her first hundred days have yielded two remarkable achievements at home. The first was a huge victory for the administration in gaining Senate ratification of

the International Chemical Weapons Treaty. The Treaty
was first conceived during the Reagan administration, and
was designed to call on the countries of the world to cease
the production and the use of chemical weapons. Despite
the fact that it was negotiated and signed by President
Bush, it had been bogged down by largely conservative
forces in the Senate, which objected to specific verification
components. But more than that, the truly offensive aspect
of the Treaty to its opponents was the concept of "unilateral disarmament," given that outlaw nations such as Iraq
and Libya have long refused to participate in the International Chemical Weapons Conference and would never
sign or abide by the terms of the treaty. Ironically, the
biggest opponent of the Treaty was the senior senator from
North Carolina.

For months Secretary Albright and the administration
mounted a concerted lobbying effort, counting Generals
Shalikashvili, Norman Schwarzkopf, and Colin Powell
among their primary supporters on this issue. As she made
the rounds on the Hill and the talk-show circuit, the Secretary emphatically made the point that "We cannot allow
the rule-breaker to make the rules. We are trying to get
some control over this, the deadliest of all weapons of mass
destruction!" Put more simply, Albright admonished her
opponents that for "the United States to fail to ratify the
Treaty is to align ourselves with Saddam Hussein." Weeks
passed and negotiations grew more contentious. Despite
this, a final vote on the matter was scheduled for April 29.
As the deadline grew closer, Albright urged the White
House to offer Helms some procedural concessions

on the Treaty, including the ability of the United States to opt out of the agreement for reasons of noncompliance by fellow signatories or other specific strategic imperatives. This apparently did the trick, mollifying the conservative opposition, as the full Senate delivered the sixty-seven votes necessary for ratification before the deadline. Finally, the Chemical Weapons Treaty, a pact that 160 nations had signed, countless military leaders had supported, and for which three separate US presidents had lobbied vigorously over a twenty-year period, had become law.

Although some may argue that ratification of the Chemical Weapons Treaty represents the brass ring of Madeleine Albright's first hundred days, many familiar with the landscape surrounding Foggy Bottom will argue vehemently that the long-awaited State Department Reorganization, authorized by President Clinton on April 17, 1997, was Albright's crowning achievement to date. As any observer of the diplomatic scene will attest, for more than three decades the issue as to who truly oversees US foreign policy has festered both on Capitol Hill as well as throughout the halls of State. The issue has outlasted Presidents Nixon, Ford, Carter, Reagan, and Bush. Other disputes such as foreign aid, the United Nations, as well as certain humanitarian and prodemocracy initiatives, have, in truth, simply been by-products of this mammoth controversy. The battle lines have been clear for years. Foreign policy hawks wanted the independent agencies reeled in or eliminated. On the opposite side were globalists who were staunchly opposed to either option. Fortuitously, the timing was right. Some have alleged that it may have been a concession to win support for the Chemical Weapons Treaty or perhaps a maneuver to propel the Foreign Relations Committee chairman to acquiesce on the issue of the United States' long outstanding dues at the United Nations. But whatever the reason, on that April day a logjam of Herculean proportions was broken as the State Department Reorganization Plan was approved. Effectively, the plan merges the State Department, the Arms Control and Disarmament Agency, and the US Information Agency, with State retaining control and supervisory authority over both entities. While the Agency for International Development would remain independent, it would be subject to significantly greater oversight by the Department of State.

From a purely political standpoint, it is telling that the conservative forces accepted a deal that provided greater accountability and oversight in lieu of total elimination. The globalists accepted it to insure the agencies' very survival. Notwithstanding the motivation, most observers agree that the end result will be a leaner, more efficient, and more accountable foreign policy apparatus, operating under the helm of Secretary of State Madeleine Albright.

In assessing the accomplishments of Madeleine Albright's first one hundred days in office one would be remiss to ignore the clear impact resulting from the sheer force of her personality. On the streets of Washington and New York, Albright is rarely greeted with the deferential salutation of "Madam Secretary," but more often with something to the effect of "Hey, Madeleine!" As she is the first to admit, this instantaneous familiarity on the part of total strangers should not be perceived as a sign of disrespect. Rather, it is quite similar to familiar overtures such as "Go, Michael," from basketball fans, "You-da-Man, Shark," from golfers, "Bru-u-u-ce!" from aficionados of rock 'n' roll, or "Arnold!" from fans of action films. Moreover, for Albright, this phenomenon has been repeated time and time again in such disparate locales as Prague, Sarajevo, Helsinki, Moscow, Tokyo, Beijing, London, Paris, Munich, Santiago, Mexico City, Guatemala City, and Baltimore, where she dazzled the opening day crowd by throwing out the first ball to start the Orioles' season—dressed in the team's cap and jacket, of course.

In essence, what Secretary of State Madeleine Albright has done is to somehow put US foreign policy on a first-name basis with the rest of the world. To thousands, perhaps millions, of people whom she will never meet, whose vision of this country is based only on what they read in papers or see on television, she symbolizes what we stand for. She alone makes the first impression. For the first time, instead of seeing a middle-aged white man in a dull suit, they see a grandmother in a flak jacket, someone whom people flock to see like a rock star.

Internationally, one has to go back to the days of JFK to witness this kind of a personal connection with this nation's role in the world. Back then, Peace Corps volunteers used to tell of going into primitive villages in Africa or South America, with no running water or electricity, only to enter the hut of a villager and find a picture of President Kennedy tacked to a wall. As amazing as it sounds, thirty years ago, the dream of this country's promise, its potential, had that effect on people. But that somehow ended with Kennedy's assassination and the escalation of the Cold War. For more than thirty years, the superpower sitting between Canada and Mexico was known as this huge, impersonal, monolithic entity called the United States.

But since Madeleine Albright took office as this country's Secretary of State, her adopted homeland is, for the first time in thirty years, once again being referred to by the rest of the world as "America."

SOURCES

NOTE TO THE READER: Please be advised that some accounts of conversations contained in *Madam Secretary* were reconstructed based on multiple versions provided by third parties.

*   *   *

Anne Albright, Q & A, March 12, 1997, April 3, 1997.

Madeleine Albright, UN Ambassador-Designate, statement at confirmation hearing before Senate Foreign Relations Committee, Jan. 21, 1993.

Madeleine Albright, Secretary of State-Designate, statement before the Senate Foreign Relations Committee, Jan. 8, 1997.

Madeleine Albright, interview by Larry King, *Larry King Live* (CNN), Jan. 25, 1997.

Madeleine Albright, interview by Tim Russert, *Meet the Press* (NBC), Jan. 26, 1997.

Madeleine Albright, interview by Ed Bradley, *Sixty Minutes* (CBS), February 9, 1997.

Madeleine Albright, interview by Sam Donaldson, Cokie Roberts, and George Will, *This Week* (ABC), Feb. 23, 1997.

Madeleine Albright, interview by Jim Lehrer, *The News Hour with Jim Lehrer* (PBS), March 6, 1997.

Madeleine Albright, interview by Bob Schieffer and Tom Friedman, *Face the Nation* (CBS), March 23, 1997.

Madeleine Albright and Jesse Helms, press briefing at Wingate University, Wingate, N.C., March 25, 1997.

Madeleine Albright, interview by Diane Rehm, *The Diane Rehm Show* (WAMU-FM), March 27, 1997.

Madeleine Albright, statement before the Senate Foreign Relations Committee on chemical weapons convention, April 8, 1997.

Madeleine Albright, interviews on chemical weapons, Satellite TV Tour, April 18, 1997.

Madeleine Albright, interview by Tim Russert and Andrea Mitchell, *Meet the Press* (NBC), April 20, 1997.

Madeleine Albright, statement before the Senate Armed Services Committee on NATO enlargement, April 23, 1997.

Madeleine Albright, press briefing en route to Moscow, April 30, 1997.

Madeleine Albright, interview by Dan Rather, *CBS Evening News* (CBS), May 14, 1997.

Atlanta Constitution, Jan. 23, 1997, Sec. A, p. 6, "Albright faces potpourri of issues at home, abroad," Bob Deans.

Lauren Battaglia, interview, March 3, 1997.

Leon Billings, interview, April 16, 1997.

Thomas Blood and Bruce Henderson, *State of the Union: A Report on President Clinton's First Four Years in Office* (Santa Monica, Cal.: General Publishing Group, 1996).

Boston Globe, June 8, 1995, Sec. A, p. 23, "US envoy to UN is said to harden Serb stance." Colum Lynch, Dusko Doder.

Boston Globe, Aug. 11, 1995, Sec. A, p. 1, "US links rebel Serbs to possible massacre," Colum Lynch.

Boston Globe, Dec. 16, 1995, Sec. A, p. 9, "UN Chief, Albright engage in squabble," Colum Lynch.

Boston Globe, Dec. 20, 1995, Sec. A, p. 17, "Serbian account of massacre hit," Colum Lynch.

Boston Globe, March 22, 1996, Sec. A, p. 2, "Angry Serbs jeer Albright in Croatia."

Boston Globe, Dec. 12, 1996, Sec. A, p. 27, "Albright's new perspective on the world," Ellen Goodman.

Boston Globe, Jan 9, 1997, Sec. A, p. 2, "Albright breezes through hearing," David Marcus.

Barbara Boxer, senator, Q & A, April 22, 1997.

Chicago Tribune, June 26, 1995, Sec. 1, p. 11, "Happy anniversary: UN still is in America's best interest," Madeleine Albright.

Chicago Tribune, March 23, 1996, Sec. 1, p. 3, "Grisly visit to Bosnia's killing fields," Tom Hundley.

Chicago Tribune, Dec. 6, 1996, Sec. 1, p. 1, "U.N. Envoy made her mark with a blunt style," Terry Atlas.

Chicago Tribune, Jan. 9, 1997, Sec. 1, p. 3, "Albright's diplomacy a hit on the Hill," Terry Atlas.

Chicago Tribune, Jan. 25, 1997, Sec. 1, p. 3, "NATO expansion, China, top issues on her 1st full day," David Cloud.

Christian Science Monitor, Aug. 18, 1995, p. 4, "Albright defends U.S. role at China conclave," George Moffett.

Christian Science Monitor, Feb. 1, 1996, p. 7, "Halting Rwanda-style tragedies," George Moffett.

Christian Science Monitor, Jan. 30, 1997, p. 1, "U.S.-European ties emerge from era of the big chill," Jonathan Landay.

Warren Christopher, former Secretary of State, interview, April 10, 1997.

Bill Clinton, remarks at announcement of new cabinet officers, Dec. 5, 1996.

Bill Clinton, remarks at swearing-in ceremony, January 23, 1997.

Kent Conrad, senator, Q & A, April 22, 1997.

Current Biography, vol. 56, issue 5, May 1995, p. 6–11, "Madeleine Korbel Albright."

James Davidson, interview, March 31, 1997.

Geraldine Ferraro, interview, May 7, 1997.

Foreign Affairs, vol. 73, issue 1, Jan. 1994, pp. 56–66, "Wrong turn in Somalia," John Bolton.

Foreign Affairs, vol. 74, issue 6, Nov. 1995, p. 141, Gail Gerhart, "Africa— Losing Mogadishu," review of *Testing U.S. Policy in Somalia,* by Jonathan Stevenson.

Foreign Affairs, vol. 76, issue 2, March/April 1997, p. 170, "Richard Holbrooke on Bosnia," Richard Holbrooke.

Dick Gephardt (D. Mo.), House minority leader, interview, April 16, 1997.

Gail Griffith, interview, April 16, 1997.

Peter Kelley, interview, April 9, 1997.

Bob Kerrey, (D. Neb.), senator, interview, April 23, 1997.

Dean Peter Krough, interview, April 11, 1997.

Patrick Leahy, senator, interview, April 23, 1997.

Elliott Levitas, interview, March 1997.

Los Angeles Times, Aug. 11, 1995, Sec. A, p. 12, "Photos show mass graves of civilians from 'safe areas,' U.S. tells U.N."

Los Angeles Times, Sept. 7, 1995, Sec. A, p. 14, "U.S. presses China on rights; Abortion battle averted."

Los Angeles Times, Dec. 16, 1995, Sec. A, p. 6, "Despite its own little war, U.N. okays Bosnia mission," Stanley Meisler.

Los Angeles Times, Feb. 28, 1996, Sec. A, p. 1, "Cubans gleeful, U.S. transcript of attack shows," Stanley Meisler.

Los Angeles Times, Dec. 6, 1996, Sec. A, p. 1, "Albright is team player, tough fighter," Stanley Meisler.

Los Angeles Times, Jan. 9, 1997, Sec. A, p. 18, "Albright offers her agenda to receptive Senate panel," Tyler Marshall.

Los Angeles Times, Jan. 25, 1997, Sec. A, p. 6, "Albright to chart new course in foreign policy," Tyler Marshall.

Barbara Mikulski, senator, interview, April 22, 1997.

The Nation, vol. 263, number 22, Dec. 30, 1996, p. 3, "Helmswoman at State."

The New Republic, vol. 211, issue 8–9, Aug. 22, 1994, pp. 19–27, "Albright's mission," Jacob Heilbraun, Carol Giacomo.

The New York Times, July 26, 1988, Sec. A, p. 16, "Dukakis foreign policy advisor: Madeleine Korbel Albright," Elaine Sciolino.

The New York Times, Dec. 23, 1992, Sec. A, p. 14, "Clinton's new foreign policy thinkers: like-minded ex-Carter teammates."

The New York Times, August 10, 1993, Sec. A, p. 19, "Yes, there is a reason to be in Somalia," Madeleine Albright.

The New York Times, June 25, 1994, Sec. A, p. 5, "U.S. will seek voluntary curbs on North Korea arms deal," Michael Gordon.

The New York Times, Oct. 18, 1994, Sec. A, p. 1, "U.S. criticizes a Russian aide at U.N. on Iraq," Elaine Sciolino.

The New York Times, Nov. 15, 1994, Sec. A, p. 6, "The U.N. Security Council decides to keep economic sanctions on Iraq," Richard D. Lyons.

The New York Times, Nov. 25, 1994, Sec. A, p. 1, "Albright makes her U.N. post a focal point," Barbara Crossette.

The New York Times, Aug. 6, 1995, Sec. 1, p. 6, "U.S. upholds role at talks on women," Barbara Crossette.

The New York Times, Nov. 19, 1995, Sec. C, p. 1, "We won't let war criminals walk," Madeleine Albright.

The New York Times, Feb. 22, 1996, Sec. A, p. 6, "In an about-face, U.S. proposes standby force for Burundi," Barbara Crossette.

The New York Times, March 22, 1996, Sec. A, p. 3, "Serbs stone Albright's motorcade."

The New York Times, Sept. 22, 1996, Sec. C, p. 63, "Madeleine Albright's audition," Elaine Sciolino.

The New York Times, Dec. 6, 1996, Sec. A, p. 1, "A political diplomat: Madeleine Korbel Albright," Barbara Crossette.

The New York Times, Dec. 6, 1996, Sec. B, p. B, "Selection for Secretary of State is praised by Helms and others," Steven Erlanger.

The New York Times, Dec. 19, 1996, Sec. A, p. 29, "Madeleine Albright's Munich mindset," Owen Harries.

The New York Times, Jan. 1, 1997, Sec. A, p. 3, "Boutros-Ghali's query to Albright: 'What went wrong?' "

The New York Times, Jan. 23, 1997, Sec. A, p. 22, "Madeleine Albright's Agenda," editorial.

The New York Times, Jan. 25, 1997, Sec. A, p. 4, "Albright vows to seek support in U.S. for Clinton foreign policy," Steven Erlanger.

The New York Times, May 14, 1997, Sec. A, p. 10, "Winning friends for foreign policy: Albright's first 100 days," Steven Erlanger.

The New Yorker, vol. 71, issue 30, Oct. 2, 1995, p. 35, "The Talk of the Town: Albright throws the book at Powell," David Remnick.

Newsweek, Oct. 18, 1993, pp. 34–38, "The making of a fiasco," Michael Elliott.

Newsweek, Oct. 18, 1993, pp. 39–43, "Firefight from hell," Tom Post with Daniel Pedersen.

Newsweek, Aug. 28, 1995, p. 45, "Making it hard on Hillary," Carroll Bogert, Katharine Chubbuck.

Newsweek, Sept. 4, 1995, p. 24, "Beyond Gender," Betty Friedan.

Newsweek, Sept. 11, 1995, p. 42, "Struggling through hell and high water," Russell Watson.

Newsweek, Sept. 18, 1995, p. 50, "We turned this around," Carroll Bogert.

Newsweek, August 12, 1996, pp. 68–71, "Naked mission," Col. David H. Hackworth.

Newsweek, Dec. 16, 1996, pp. 24–28, "The lady is a hawk," Mathew Cooper.

Newsweek, Feb. 10, 1997, p. 23, "One woman's journey to the top."

Newsweek, Feb. 17, 1997, p. 4, "How she found out."

Newsweek, Feb. 17, 1997 p. 44, "Making peace with the past," Kati Marton.

Newsweek, Feb. 24, 1997, p. 30, "Interview with Madeleine Albright."

People magazine, vol. 46, issue 26, Dec. 1996, pp. 46–48, "Madam Secretary," Bill Hewitt, Glenn Garelik, Maria Eftimiades.

Harry Reid, senator, interview, April 9, 1997.

Jay Rockefeller, senator, Q & A, April 22, 1997.

Time magazine, October 18, 1994, pp. 40–50, "Anatomy of a Disaster," George J. Church.

Time magazine, Oct. 31, 1994, pp. 28–34, "Taking his show on the road." George Church, Kevin Feclande.

Time magazine, vol. 149, issue 1, Dec. 16, 1996, pp. 32–33, "The voice of America," Nancy Gibbs.

Time magazine, vol 149, issue 7, Feb. 17, 1997, p. 53, "The many lives of Madeleine," Nancy Gibbs, Ann Blackman, and Douglas Waller.

USA Today, Jan. 27, 1993, Sec. A, p. 8, "Pickering tapped for Russia Post; Albright OK'd for U.N.," Michael Katz.

USA Today, April 8, 1993, Sec. A, p. 6, "U.N. Ambassador lives a tale of two cities," Michael Katz.

USA Today, Aug. 4, 1994, Sec. A, p. 8, "Pan Am 103: Don't ease pressure on Libya," Madeleine Albright.

USA Today, Feb. 24, 1995, Sec. A, p. 4, "U.S. on a mission to maintain Iraq embargo," Michael Katz.

USA Today, Aug. 30, 1995, Sec. A, p. 11, "Forum's Value: Waste of money or time to bond?" Marilyn Greene.

USA Today, Sept. 16, 1996, Sec. A, p. 1, "U.S. wary of Saddam vow."

USA Today, Dec. 5, 1996, Sec. A, p. 1, "Albright tops list for State," Susan Page.

USA Today, Dec. 6, 1996, Sec. A, p. 1, "Albright tapped as first woman to head State," Susan Page.

USA Today, Dec. 6, 1996, Sec. A, p. 6, "On way to top, Albright made her own way," Michael Katz.

USA Today, Dec. 6, 1996, Sec. A, p. 8, "Fresh thinking will enhance foreign policy," Susan Page.

USA Today, Jan. 9, 1997, Sec. A, p. 10, "Hugs, kisses set hearing's tone," Michael Katz.

USA Today, May 12, 1997, Sec. A, p. 1, "Albright: Going public with diplomacy," Michael Katz.

USDS *Dispatch*, vol. 4, issue 12, March 22, 1993, pp. 166–167, "UN Security Council adopts resolution 808 on war crimes tribunal."

USDS *Dispatch*, vol. 4, issue 14, 1993, pp. 207–211, "Current status of U.S. policy, on Bosnia, Somalia, and U.N. reform." Madeleine Albright.

USDS *Dispatch*, vol. 4, issue 26, June 28, pp. 461–464, "Strong United Nations serves U.S. security interests," Madeleine Albright.

USDS *Dispatch*, vol. 4, issue 27, July 5, 1993, p. 479, "Explanation of U.S. vote on lifting arms embargo against Bosnia."

USDS Dispatch, vol 4, issue 39, Sept. 27, 1993, pp. 665–668, "The use of force in a post–Cold War world," Madeleine Albright.

USDS *Dispatch*, vol. 5, issue 16, April 18, 1994, pp. 209–212, "Bosnia in light of the Holocaust," Madeleine Albright.

USDS *Dispatch*, vol. 5, issue 26, June 27, 1994, pp. 434–437, "Realism and idealism in American foreign policy today," Madeleine Albright.

USDS *Dispatch*, vol. 5, issue 26, June 27, 1994, pp. 438–439, "The Tragedy in Rwanda: International cooperation to find a solution," Madeleine Albright.

USDS *Dispatch*, vol. 5, issue 30, July 25, 1994, pp. 493–496, "The future of the U.S.–U.N. relationship." Madeleine Albright.

USDS *Dispatch*, vol. 5, issue 45, Nov. 7, 1994, pp. 744–748, "Principle, power, and purpose in the new era," Madeleine Albright.

USDS *Dispatch*, vol. 5, issue 47, Nov. 21, 1994, pp. 780–781, "U.N. Security Council establishes international tribunal for Rwanda," Madeleine Albright.

USDS *Dispatch*, vol. 5, issue 47, Nov. 21, 1994, pp. 778–779, "U.S. support for U.N. Security Council resolution concerning Bosnia," Madeleine Albright.

USDS *Dispatch*, vol. 6, issue 6, Feb. 6. 1995, pp. 79–83, "The United States and the United Nations: Confrontation or consensus?" Madeleine Albright.

USDS *Dispatch*, vol. 6, issue 7, Feb. 13, 1995, pp. 93–94, "Keeping faith with the people of Haiti," Madeleine Albright.

USDS *Dispatch*, vol. 6, issue 27, July 3, 1995, pp. 535–537, "The U.N. at 50: Renewing the vision," Bill Clinton, Madeleine Albright, and Warren Christopher.

USDS *Dispatch*, vol. 6, issue 32, Aug. 7, 1995, pp. 625–626, "Charting further gains in the status and the rights of women," Madeleine Albright.

USDS *Dispatch*, vol. 6, issue 34, August 21, 1995, pp. 645–647, "U.N. Security Council adopts Resolution 1009 on Croatia," Madeleine Albright.

USDS *Dispatch*, vol. 6, issue 34, August 21, 1995, pp. 647–648, "U.N. Security Council adopts Resolution 1010 on Bosnian Serbs," Madeleine Albright.

USDS *Dispatch*, vol. 6, issue 34, August 21, 1995, pp. 649–653, "U.S. policy toward Iraq," Madeleine Albright.

USDS *Dispatch*, vol. 6, issue 36, Sept. 4, 1995, pp. 674–676, "Fourth U.N. Conference on Women: U.S. efforts to promote equal rights on women," Madeleine Albright.

U.S. News and World Report, Sept. 11, 1995, p. 43, "Drawing battle lines in Beijing," Susan V. Lawrence.

U.S. News and World Report, Sept, 18, 1995, p. 63, "Two Steps forward, three steps back," Emily MacFarquhar and Susan V. Lawrence.

U.S. News and World Report, Feb. 13, 1996, p. 60, "Clinton's gung-ho voice at the U.N.," Richard Chesnoff.

U.S. News and World Report, March 3, 1997, p. 9, "Small touches and big plans," Fred Coleman.

The Wall Street Journal, Aug. 11, 1995, Sec. A, p. 1, "The U.S. presented evidence of war crimes."

The Wall Street Journal, Aug. 28, 1995, Sec. A, p. 12, "Saddam's yellow rain."

The Wall Street Journal, Dec. 5, 1996, Sec. A, p. 22, "While Clinton favors Albright to run foreign policy, critics raise concerns," Michael Frisby, Robert Greenberger.

The Wall Street Journal, Dec. 16, 1996, Sec. A, p. 17, "Now, more than ever, Europe needs leadership," George Melloan.

The Wall Street Journal, Jan. 9, 1997, Sec. A, p. 14, "Albright sails through confirmation hearings," Carla Robbins, Robert Greenberger.

The Wall Street Journal, Jan. 24, 1997, Sec. A, p. 1, "Around the world."

The Wall Street Journal, Feb. 13, 1997, Sec. A, p. 19, "The smart pol who's now running Foggy Bottom."

The Washington Post, Jan. 7, 1994, Sec A, p. 14, "U.S. presses Balkan war tribunal," David Ottaway.

The Washington Post, March 31, 1994, Sec A, p. 25, "Albright, Shalikashvili signal U.S. ties to Bosnia," John Pomfret.

The Washington Post, Oct 14, 1994, Sec. A, p. 34, "U.N. Envoy Albright emerges as administration's straight talker," Julia Preston.

The Washington Post, March 5, 1995, Sec. A, p. 1, "U.S. wins votes to keep Iraq oil ban," Julia Preston.

The Washington Post, March 17, 1995, Sec. A, p. 27, "Misplaced misgivings: We are leading the United Nations, not the other way around," Madeleine Albright.

The Washington Post, May 31, 1995, Sec. B, p. 3, "The Reliable Source," Lois Romano, with Mary Welch.

The Washington Post, Nov. 15, 1996, Sec. A, p. 12, "Women press for administration posts: Coalition members meet with President."

The Washington Post, Nov. 19, 1995, Sec. C, p. 1, "We won't let war criminals walk," Madeleine Albright.

The Washington Post, Oct. 29, 1995, Sec. C, p. 2, "Settling with the enemy: The dicey politics of negotiating peace in the Balkans with accused war criminals," Gary Bass.

The Washington Post, Dec. 16, 1995, Sec. A, p. 30, "UN's normal decorous diplomatic discourse takes beating in dispute," John Goshko.

The Washington Post, Dec. 6, 1996, Sec. A, p. 1, "Clinton picks Albright for State Department," Peter Baker, John Harris.

The Washington Post, Dec. 6, 1996, Sec. A, p. 25, "Albright's personal odyssey shaped foreign policy beliefs," Michael Dobbs, John Goshko.

The Washington Post, Dec. 7, 1996, Sec. A, p. 1, "Clinton mulled every option until the end," John Harris, Michael Dobbs.

The Washington Post, Dec. 10, 1996, Sec. A, p. 19, "One Woman . . . ," E. J. Dionne.

The Washington Post, Jan. 7, 1997, Sec. A, p. 1, "Albright led challenge to U.N. chief: Success against Boutros-Ghali boosts State Department choice on Capitol Hill," Thomas Lippman, John Goshko.

The Washington Post, Jan. 9, 1997, Sec. A, p. 10, "At Albright's confirmation hearing, differences are smoothed over," Thomas Lippman.

The Washington Post, Jan. 9, 1997, Sec. A, p. 20, "Ambassador Albright on the Hill."

The Washington Post, Jan. 9, 1997, Sec. A, p. 21, "Madeleine Albright's gift," Josiah Auspitz.

The Washington Post, Jan. 24, 1997, Sec. A, p. 32, "New Secretary of State goes right to work: Albright meets with Clinton, U.N.'s Annan after taking the oath," Thomas Lippman.

The Washington Post, Jan. 25, 1997, Sec. A, p. 4, "Albright to 'tell it like it is' on human rights," Thomas Lippman.

The Washington Post, Feb. 4, 1997, Sec. A, p. 1, "Albright's family tragedy comes to light," Michael Dobbs.

The Washington Post, Feb. 4, 1997, Sec. A, p. 6, "Albright story sparks sympathy, fascination," Michael Dobbs.

The Washington Post, Feb. 7, 1997, Sec. A, p. 23, "Holocaust's child," Walter Reich.

The Washington Post Magazine, Feb. 7, 1997, p. 9, "Out of the past," Michael Dobbs.

The Washington Post, Feb. 16, 1997, Sec. A, p. 37, "Albright arrives in Rome, first stop of first trip as top U.S. Diplomat," Michael Dobbs.

The Washington Post, Feb. 16, 1997, Sec. A, p. 36, "Albright received as 'Iron Lady,' " Michael Dobbs.

The Washington Post, Feb. 23, 1997, Sec. A, p. 22, "Albright goes to Cold War outpost to press for Korean dialogue," Michael Dobbs.

The Washington Post, Feb. 23, 1997, Sec. C, p. 7, "Albright's difference," David Broder.

The Washington Post, May 2, 1997, Sec. A, p. 21, "U.S.-Russia talks on NATO charter stall," Michael Dobbs.

The Washington Post, May 16, 1997, Sec. A, p. 28, "Albright scolds top Croatian diplomat," Michael Dobbs.

The Washington Post, May 23, 1997, Sec. A, p. 27, "In the loop," Al Kamen.

The Washington Post, May 23, 1997, Sec. A, p. 33, "Albright says U.S. will not allow ethnic fighting to resume in Bosnia," Michael Dobbs.

The Washington Post, May 28, 1997, Sec. A, p. 17, "Turf diplomacy at the State Department," Stephen Barr and Thomas Lippman.

Steven Wayne, professor, Georgetown University, interview, March 1997.

Eric White, interview, March 17, 1997.

INDEX